458-457

*DETROIT STUDIES IN*
*MUSIC BIBLIOGRAPHY*

*GENERAL EDITOR*
*BRUNO NETTL*
*UNIVERSITY OF ILLINOIS AT URBANA-CHAMPAIGN*

# FIFTEEN BLACK AMERICAN COMPOSERS
## A Bibliography of Their Works

### Alice Tischler

with the assistance of
CAROL TOMASIC

DETROIT STUDIES IN MUSIC BIBLIOGRAPHY  FORTY-FIVE
Information Coordinators  1981  Detroit

Copyright © 1981 by Alice Tischler

Printed and bound in the United States of America

Published by
Information Coordinators, Inc.
1435-37 Randolph Street
Detroit, Michigan 48226

Book design by Vincent Kibildis

LIBRARY OF CONGRESS CATALOGING IN PUBLICATION DATA

Tischler, Alice.
    Fifteen Black American composers.

 ✓(Detroit studies in music bibliography ; 45)
    Includes indexes.
    Contents: Boatner, Edward Hammond — Bonds, Margaret
Allison — Clark, Edgar Rogie — [etc.]
    1. Afro-American composers—Bio-bibliography.
I. Tomasic, Carol. II. Title. III. Series.
ML106.U3T57        016.78         81-1162
ISBN 0-89990-003-8              AACR2

# CONTENTS

## INTRODUCTION

THIS VOLUME is intended to fill an important gap in the reference literature on American music. Black composers constitute a significant segment of art music in America; yet little of their large output is generally known. The present bibliography will at least make available such knowledge about a small group of men and women writing in recent decades. A similar monograph covering a limited number of composers has already appeared: *The Black Composer Speaks*, edited by David N. Baker, Lida M. Belt, and Herman C. Hudson, (New Jersey: Scarecrow Press, 1977). It is hoped that others will continue this bibliographical exposure of the many Black American composers and their output.

The present bibliography presents information about a group of Black composers primarily involved in art music. This term, viz. "art music," is, in this author's opinion, better than either "classical" or "serious" music; it implies, of course, a factor of judgment (as does even the term "music"). Here it is used for a particular type of music meant especially for the traditional concert stage, dramatic media, or church, distinguishing it from such other types as popular music, jazz, and folk music, with their many subgroupings. Although spirituals fall into the class of folk music, it is the artistic settings these composers have written which justifies their inclusion in this bibliography. Once the composer was chosen for inclusion in this bibliography on the basis of his output of "art" music, his entire production of whatever type of music was non-selectively and non-critically incorporated.

The composers were chosen chiefly because of the absence of, and therefore a need for, comprehensive documentation for them. The younger generation, represented here by Roger Dickerson, James Furman, Adolphus Hailstork, Robert Harris, Carman Moore, Dorothy Moore, and John Price, runs the gamut from conservative form and instrumentation to so-called avantgarde employing electronic sounds. In addition, several of these composers, including also Arthur Cunningham, Wendell Logan, and Frederick Tillis, make wide use of the jazz medium. Of the older generation, Edward Boatner, William Dawson, and Noah Ryder have been particularly successful with their settings of spirituals. The works of Margaret Bonds, although on the whole conservative in form and instrumentation, cover not only "art" music and spirituals but also popular music. Rogie Clark falls into a category by himself, being mainly pre-occupied with the study of negro folk music and its incorporation into "art" music.

The information assembled in this volume comes principally from primary sources. All living composers were personally contacted by this author; nine were visited, and the others, contacted by letter and/or telephone, completed detailed worksheets with information about their compositions. Additional information was secured from libraries, publishers, the Library of Congress *Catalog of Copyright Entries*, the *National Union Catalog* and numerous other publications. Information for Noah Ryder was supplied primarily by the composer's widow, Dr. Georgia Ryder, and Marjorie Johnson, both faculty members at Norfolk State College, and by the American Society of Composers, Authors, and Publishers (ASCAP). Most data for Margaret Bonds were furnished by her daughter, Djane Richardson.[1] To all these I wish to express my thanks. Even so, the bibliography is incomplete; many of the above people were unable to fully reconstruct all information requested, and it is impossible to gather complete information from reference and other sources. This is especially true with regard to Margaret Bonds and Edward Boatner. The latter composed over one hundred spirituals which are in his possession in manuscript form, a listing of which was unobtainable. Similarly, efforts to complete information about Rogie Clark, who died suddenly in 1978, have proved fruitless by the time of this writing.

The entry for each composer opens with a biographical sketch, and is followed by a list of sources used to compile the information, which may also serve for further study. The sigla for sources appearing in these lists are given in the bibliography following this Introduction. Sources which merely mention the composer are not noted. A bibliography of published and unpublished works, in alphabetical order and numbered, completes the entry. Collections of works are included in the alphabetical order but are not numbered.

---

[1] Anyone desiring information about either of these two composers may contact Dr. Georgia Ryder, Norfolk State College, Norfolk, Virginia 23504, and Djane Richardson, 501 W. 123rd St., Apt. 4B, New York, New York 10027.

Thirteen areas of information were considered for the catalog of works:

1. TITLE.

2. YEAR OF COMPOSITION.

   If known, the year is given in parentheses. In some instances, that date was not ascertainable. However, in many cases, it can be assumed that the publication or copyright date reflects the approximate date of composition. Unfortunately, that date also was sometimes unobtainable.

3. MEDIUM OF PERFORMANCE.

4. AUTHOR OF TEXT, WHERE APPLICABLE.

   It is understood that different versions of a work use the same text; therefore this information is given only with the first version.

5. COMMISSION.

6. DEDICATION.

7. PUBLICATION INFORMATION.

8. LIBRARY OR LIBRARIES HOLDING THIS SCORE.

   According to available catalogs, the libraries are noted in sigla, as follows:

   | | |
   |---|---|
   | AU | Atlanta University, Negro Collection |
   | HU | Howard University, Arthur B. Spingarn Collection of Negro Authors |
   | ILL | University of Illinois |
   | IU | Indiana University, Music Library, Black Music Collection |
   | LC | Library of Congress |
   | NYPL | New York Public Library |

9. DURATION.

   The duration of a work is given only for the first of several versions in a similar medium; for most spirituals, duration is omitted. Timings for the works of Dawson were obtained from recordings.

10. CONTENTS OF COLLECTIONS AND PARTS OF SECTIONAL WORKS.

11. FIRST PERFORMANCE.

    In most cases, the absence of first performance information indicates that there has been no performance of the particular work. However, for Margaret Bonds and Noah Ryder this information was unobtainable except when information about first performances was found in programs, reviews, or other sources. For arrangements of spirituals, performance information is omitted as not particularly instructive since spirituals are widely and often performed.

12. RECORDING INFORMATION.

> Included here is an indication of the presence of a recording in the record library of the School of Music at Indiana University. This library has a large Black music collection of both tapes and records. It is further augmented by tapes of numerous performances of Black music which are held at Indiana University. Any tape of a noncopyrighted performance can be secured from the library as can tapes of commercial recordings no longer under copyright. Indication of this library's large holdings in recordings and scores of Black music and their availability was felt to be helpful to the reader.

13. NOTES ABOUT THE WORK.

Three appendices complete this volume: a title index, a classification index, and a list of publishers used by the composers presented here with their current addresses.

# BIBLIOGRAPHY

**An**    **Anderson, E. Ruth,** comp. *Contemporary American Composers: A Biographical Dictionary.* Boston, Mass.: G. K. Hall, 1976.

**ASCAP**    **American Society of Composers, Authors and Publishers.** *The ASCAP Biographical Dictionary.* New York: American Society of Composers, 1948, 1952, 1966.

**Ba**    **Baker, Theodore.** *Biographical Dictionary of Musicians.* 5th ed. New York: Schirmer (1958); suppl. 1965.

**Cl**    **Claghorn, Charles Eugene.** *Biographical Dictionary of American Music.* West Nyack, N. Y.: Parker, 1973.

**DeR**    **DeLerma, Dominque-René.** *Reflections on Afro-American Music.* Ohio: Kent State Press, 1973.

**Ha**    **Handy, William C.** *Negro Authors and Composers of the United States.* New York: Handy Bros., n.d.

**Har**    **Hare, Maud Cuney.** *Negro Musicians and Their Music.* Washington, D. C.: Associated Publications, c1936.

**I-Who**    *International Who's Who in Music,* 1914-

**Ja**   **Jacobi, Hugh Wm.** *Contemporary American Composers, based at American Colleges and Universities.* Paradise, Calif.: Paradise Arts, 1975.

**NYB**   *Negro Year Book,* 1913- . Edited by Work, and others, Tuskegee Institute.

**Ro**   **Roach, Hildred.** *Black American Music: Past and Present.* Boston: Crescendo Publishing Co., 1973.

**Rob**   **Robinson, Wilhelmena S.** "Historical Negro Biographies." In *International Library of Negro Life and History.* New York: Publishers Co., c1968.

**SoA**   **Southern, Eileen.** "America's Black Composers of Classical Music." In *Music Educator's Journal.* November 1975, pp. 46-59.

**SoM**   **Southern, Eileen.** *The Music of Black Americans: A History.* New York: Norton, c1971.

**SoR**   **Southern, Eileen,** comp. *Readings in Black American Music.* New York: Norton, c1971.

**Th**   **Thompson, Oscar.** *The International Cyclopedia of Music and Musicians.* New York: Dodd, Mead and Co., 1944, 1949, 1964, 1975.

**To**   *Tones and Overtones; Saluting Negro Composers.* Spring 1954.

**Wh**   **White, Evelyn.** *Selected Bibliography of Published Choral Music By Black Composers.* Washington, D.C.: Howard University, 1975.

**Who-A**   *Who's Who Among Black Americans.* 2nd ed. 1977-78. Northbrook, Ill., c1978.

**Who-C**   *Who's Who in Colored America.* Edited by Fleming and Burchel. New York: Burchel and Assoc., 1928-29, 1930-32, 1933-37, 1938-40, 1941-44, 1950, 1951.

**Wi**   **Williams, Ora.** *American Black Women in the Arts and Social Sciences: A Bibliographic Survey.* New Jersey: Scarecrow, 1978.

*FIFTEEN BLACK AMERICAN COMPOSERS*
*A Bibliography of Their Works*

*Edward Boatner*

## EDWARD HAMMOND BOATNER
*b. New Orleans, Louisiana, November 13, 1897*


Boatner was the son of a traveling minister. His interest in music, spirituals in particular, was stimulated by the contacts he made with Negro folksinging in his early teens during trips he made across the country with his father. With his mother's support, he soon began piano studies.

The youth auditioned for a voice teacher at the University of Missouri who predicted a brilliant future for the young man, regretting that Boatner could not be admitted to that university, then all white. However, he was accepted at Western University in Quindara, Kansas in 1916. His interest in the Negro spiritual persisted. Shortly afterwards he sang for Roland Hayes in Kansas City, and a scholarship was arranged for the young man at the Boston Conservatory where he entered in 1921. After graduation, he attended the Longy School of Music in Boston. It was during this period that he met Robert Nathaniel Dett with whom he established a unique relationship. From Dett he received instruction in new vocal arrangements of spirituals. He continued his association with Dett as guest singer at Hampton Institute and as his soloist on tours. In 1932, Boatner graduated from the Chicago College of Music.

From 1925 to 1933, he served as Music Director of the National Baptist Convention, although much time between 1926 and 1930 was spent on concert tours where he established his reputation as an outstanding baritone. Later he was Dean of Music at Wiley College and taught at Samuel Houston College, both in Texas, before opening the Edward Boatner Studio in New York City where he teaches voice, theory, sight-singing, harmony, composition, and opera in German, Italian, and French. Some of his pupils were Josephine Baker, Libby Holman, George Shirley, and Clifton Webb.

He met Harry Burleigh at the recording studios of Geroge W. Broom where Boatner established himself as one of the first singers to record the spiritual. His arrangements of more than two hundred spirituals have appeared in the repertoires of Marian Anderson, Roland Hayes, Leontyne Price, George Shirley, Josephine Baker, Paul Robeson, Nelson Eddy, and many other singers. The forty-four voice Boatner Spiritual Chorale is a tribute to Boatner's skill as an arranger of spirituals.

For his services to music, he has won awards from the National Federation of Music Clubs, the National Association of Negro Musicians, the Brooklyn Lyceum, the Detroit Association of Musicians, the New York Uptown Musicians, and other organizations. In February 1979, the Chicago Music Association of the National Association of Negro Musicians honored him for his many years of service to music.

Along with composing and teaching, Boatner has written twenty textbooks on harmony, theory, and composition based on his experience as a teacher. In addition to the almost one-hundred works recorded here, he has written over one-hundred more spirituals which are in manuscript in his library. His output also includes pedagogical works, plays, music for stage works, and novels. He wrote a piano self-study course, which was published by Hammond Music and compiled and published several books of his arrangements of spirituals. Recent endeavors soon to be published are: *Great Achievements Black and White*, a work paralleling the accomplishments of persons of both the white and black races in all fields; *The Damaging Results of Racism*—"Love Thy Neighbor as Thyself"; *Black Humor*; and a novel, *One Drop of Blood.*

*Sources:*

> Information submitted by composer
> ASCAP 1966
> *Chicago Defender*, "Accent" section, Saturday, January 27, 1979
> Cl
> *The Crusader* (Chicago), Saturday, February 3, 1979
> Har
> "The Music Master," introduction to *Thirty Afro-American*
>     *Choral Spirituals*, collected and arranged by Edward Boatner
>     (New York: Hammond Music, 1964)
> *New York Times*, September 30, 1971, p. 49
> Program notes
> SoM
> Wh

## AFRO-AMERICAN CHORAL SPIRITUALS, THIRTY
For chorus (SATB), unaccompanied

> *Text:*
>> Spiritual
>
> *Publication:*
>> New York: Hammond Music, 1964 (AU; IU; LC)
>
> *Contents:*
>> 1. Done Made My Vow
>> 2. Ain't That Good News
>> 3. City Called Heaven
>> 4. See the Four and Twenty Elders
>> 5. Hush, Hush
>> 6. You Got to Reap
>> 7. Hold On
>> 8. My God is So High
>> 9. Oh, What a Beautiful City
>> 10. Swing Low Sweet Chariot
>> 11. I Know the Lord Laid His Hands on Me
>> 12. On Ma Journey
>> 13. I've Been 'Buked
>> 14. Lost Sheep
>> 15. Joshua
>> 16. That Gettin' Up Mornin'
>> 17. Create Me a Body
>> 18. He is King of Kings
>> 19. Let Us Break Bread Together
>> 20. Don't Feel No Ways Tired
>> 21. My Time is Come
>> 22. They Led My Lord Away
>> 23. Calvary
>> 24. He Arose
>> 25. Were You There?
>> 26. Rise and Shine
>> 27. Behold That Star
>> 28. Go Tell It on the Mountain
>> 29. Rise Up Shepherds and Follow
>> 30. New Born
>
> *Note:*
>> American Festival of Negro Arts inaugural publication

## AIN'T GOT WEARY YET. *See* I AIN'T GOT WEARY YET

**1a** AIN'T THAT GOOD NEWS (1940). *See* **THIRTY AFRO-AMERICAN CHORAL SPIRITUALS,** no. 2

**1b** AIN'T THAT GOOD NEWS (1944). *See* **THE STORY OF THE SPIRITUALS,** no. 1; **SIXTEEN SOLO SPIRITUALS FOR VOICE AND PIANO,** no. 2

**2** AIN'T YOU GLAD (1927). *See* **SPIRITUALS TRIUMPHANT OLD AND NEW,** no. 1

**3** ALL O' MY SINS (1927). *See* **SPIRITUALS TRIUMPHANT OLD AND NEW,** no. 2

**4** THE ANGEL ROLLED THE STONE AWAY (1927)
For chorus (SATB), unaccompanied
> *Text:*
>> Spiritual
> *Publication:*
>> New York: Ricordi, 1954 (IU; LC; HU)

**5a** BABY BETHLEHEM (1927)
For chorus (SATB) and solo vocal quartet, unaccompanied
> *Text:*
>> Spiritual
> *Publication:*
>> New York: Colombo, 1964 (IU; LC)

**5b** BABY BETHLEHEM (1944). *See* **THE STORY OF THE SPIRITUALS,** no. 2

**6** BALM IN GILEAD (1927). *See* **SPIRITUALS TRIUMPHANT OLD AND NEW,** no. 3

**7** BEHOLD THAT STAR (1927). *See* **THIRTY AFRO-AMERICAN CHORAL SPIRITUALS,** no. 27

8    BY(E) AND BY(E) (1944). *See* THE STORY OF THE SPIRITUALS, no. 3;
     SIXTEEN SOLO SPIRITUALS FOR VOICE AND PIANO, no. 5

9    CALVARY (1927). *See* THIRTY AFRO-AMERICAN CHORAL SPIRITUALS,
     no. 23

10   CAN I RIDE? (1927). *See* SPIRITUALS TRIUMPHANT OLD AND NEW, no. 4

11   CERTAINLY LORD (1927). *See* SPIRITUALS TRIUMPHANT OLD AND NEW,
     no. 5

12   CHILDREN, DON'T GET WEARY (1927). *See* SPIRITUALS TRIUMPHANT
     OLD AND NEW, no. 6

13a  CITY CALLED HEAVEN (1943). *See also* THIRTY AFRO-AMERICAN
     CHORAL SPIRITUALS, no. 3
     For chorus (SATB), unaccompanied
          *Dedication:*
               To Carl Diton
          *Publication:*
               New York: Hammond Music, 1952 (IU)

13b  CITY CALLED HEAVEN (1944). *See* THE STORY OF THE SPIRITUALS,
     no. 4; SIXTEEN SOLO SPIRITUALS FOR VOICE AND PIANO, no. 6

14   COULDN'T HEAR NOBODY PRAY (1927). *See* SPIRITUALS TRIUMPHANT
     OLD AND NEW, no. 7

15   CREATE ME A BODY (1964). *See also* THIRTY AFRO-AMERICAN CHORAL
     SPIRITALS, no. 17

16a  THE CRUCIFIXION (1927). *See also* SPIRITUALS TRIUMPHANT OLD AND
     NEW, no. 8
     For chorus (SATB), unaccompanied

*Dedication:*
　　To Nora Holt
*Publication:*
　　New York: Hammond Music, 1953 (IU)

**16b**　**THE CRUCIFIXION (1944).** *See* **THE STORY OF THE SPIRITUALS**, no. 5; **SIXTEEN SOLO SPIRITUALS FOR VOICE AND PIANO**, no. 12

**17**　**DIDN'T MY LORD DELIVER DANIEL? (1944).** *See* **THE STORY OF THE SPIRITUALS**, no. 6

**18a**　**DONE MADE MY VOW (1944).** *See* **THIRTY AFRO-AMERICAN CHORAL SPIRITUALS**, no. 1

**18b**　**DONE MADE MY VOW (1944).** *See* **THE STORY OF THE SPIRITUALS**, no. 7; **SIXTEEN SOLO SPIRITUALS FOR VOICE AND PIANO**, no. 1

**19**　**DON'T FEEL NO WAYS TIRED (1944).** *See* **THIRTY AFRO-AMERICAN CHORAL SPIRITUALS**, no. 20

**20**　**DOWN BY THE RIVERSIDE (1927).** *See* **SPIRITUALS TRIUMPHANT OLD AND NEW**, no. 9

**21**　**EVENING STAR WILL GUIDE ME (ca. 1938)**
For voice and piano
　　　*Text:*
　　　　　By James Scott
　　　*Unpublished*

**22**　**FREEDOM SUITE—RISE AND SHINE (1960)**
For large chorus (SATB), orchestra, and narrator
　　　*Text:*
　　　　　By Rudolf Schramm

*Dedication:*
    To Lyndon Johnson
*Publication:*
    New York: Hammond Music, 1966 (score) (LC; HU)
*First performance:*
    April 2, 1967; Washington, D.C.; Constitution Hall; Arlington
        Symphony Orchestra
*Notes:*
    Symphonic presentation of the Negro's struggle for freedom.
    Review in *New York Times*, April 4, 1967, p. 38.


**23a  GIVE ME JESUS**
For chorus (SATB), unaccompanied

    *Text:*
        Spiritual
    *Dedication:*
        To Geroge Kemmer and the St. George's Choir
    *Publication:*
        New York: Hammond Music, 1952 (IU)


**23b  GIVE ME JESUS (1944).** *See* **THE STORY OF THE SPIRITUALS**, no. 8


**24  GIVE ME YOUR HAND (1927).** *See* **SPIRITUALS TRIUMPHANT OLD AND NEW**, no. 10


**25  GIVE ME YOUR HAND (1944).** *See* **THE STORY OF THE SPIRITUALS**, no. 9


**26  GLORY, GLORY, HALLELUJAH (1927).** *See* **SPIRITUALS TRIUMPHANT OLD AND NEW**, no. 11


**27  GO DOWN MOSES (1944).** *See* **THE STORY OF THE SPIRITUALS**, no. 10


**28a  GO TELL IT ON THE MOUNTAIN (1944).** *See* **THIRTY AFRO-AMERICAN CHORAL SPIRITUALS**, no. 28

**28b** **GO TELL IT ON THE MOUNTAIN (1944).** *See* **THE STORY OF THE SPIRITUALS,** no. 11; **SIXTEEN SOLO SPIRITUALS FOR VOICE AND PIANO,** no. 15

**29** **GOD'S GOING TO SET THIS WORLD ON FIRE (1927).** *See* **SPIRITUALS TRIUMPHANT OLD AND NEW,** no. 12

**30** **GOOD NEWS (1927).** *See* **SPIRITUALS TRIUMPHANT OLD AND NEW,** no. 13

**31** **HE AROSE (1944).** *See* **THIRTY AFRO-AMERICAN CHORAL SPIRITUALS,** no. 24

**32** **HE IS KING OF KINGS (1927).** *See* **THIRTY AFRO-AMERICAN CHORAL SPIRITUALS,** no. 18

**33** **HEAVEN'S GATE CHOIR**

> *Theater piece based on spirituals*
> *Never orchestrated*
> *Unpublished*

**34a** **HE'S GOT THE WHOLE WORLD IN HIS HANDS (1927).** *See also* **SPIRITUALS TRIUMPHANT OLD AND NEW,** no. 14
For chorus (SATB), unaccompanied

> *Publication:*
> New York: Emanuel A. Middleton, 1968 (IU)

**34b** **HE'S GOT THE WHOLE WORLD IN HIS HANDS (1944).** *See* **THE STORY OF THE SPIRITUALS,** no. 12

**35** **HIS NAME SO SWEET (1944).** *See* **THE STORY OF THE SPIRITUALS,** no. 13

**36** **HOLD ON (1927).** *See* **THIRTY AFRO-AMERICAN CHORAL SPIRITUALS,** no. 7

**37**    **HOW DID YOU FEEL? (1927).** *See* **SPIRITUALS TRIUMPHANT OLD AND NEW,** no. 15

**38**    **HUSH, HUSH (1927).** *See* **THIRTY AFRO-AMERICAN CHORAL SPIRITUALS,** no. 5; **SPIRITUALS TRIUMPHANT OLD AND NEW,** no. 16

**39**    **I AIN'T GOT WEARY YET (1944).** *See* **THE STORY OF THE SPIRITUALS,** no. 14; **SIXTEEN SOLO SPIRITUALS FOR VOICE AND PIANO,** no. 8

**40a**    **I KNOW THE LORD LAID HIS HANDS ON ME (1927).** *See* **THIRTY AFRO-AMERICAN CHORAL SPIRITUALS,** no. 11; **SPIRITUALS TRIUMPHANT OLD AND NEW,** no. 17

**40b**    **I KNOW THE LORD LAID HIS HANDS ON ME (1944).** *See* **THE STORY OF THE SPIRITUALS,** no. 15; **SIXTEEN SOLO SPIRITUALS FOR VOICE AND PIANO,** no. 14

**41**    **I SHALL NOT BE MOVED (1927).** *See* **SPIRITUALS TRIUMPHANT OLD AND NEW,** no. 18

**42a**    **I WANT JESUS TO WALK WITH ME (1944)**
For chorus (SATB), unaccompanied

> *Text:*
>> Spiritual
> *Publication:*
>> New York: Galaxy, 1949 (IU; LC)

**42b**    **I WANT JESUS TO WALK WITH ME (1936)**
For voice and piano

> *Publication:*
>> New York: Galaxy, 1939 (HU)
> *Recording:*
>> RCA Victor LSC-2592 (1962)

**43**  **I'M A SOLDIER (1927).** *See* **SPIRITUALS TRIUMPHANT OLD AND NEW,** no. 19

**44**  **I'M SO GLAD (1927).** *See* **SPIRITUALS TRIUMPHANT OLD AND NEW,** no. 20

**45**  **I'M TROUBLED IN MIND (1944).** *See* **THE STORY OF THE SPIRITUALS,** no. 16

**46**  **IN BRIGHT MANSIONS (1927)**
For chorus (SATB), solo voices, unaccompanied

>    *Text:*
>>       Spiritual
>    *Publication:*
>>       New York: Colombo, 1964 (LC)

**47**  **IN MY FATHER'S HOUSE (1927).** *See* **SPIRITUALS TRIUMPHANT OLD AND NEW,** no. 21

**48**  **I'VE BEEN 'BUKED (1960).** *See* **THIRTY AFRO-AMERICAN CHORAL SPIRITUALS,** no. 13

**49**  **I'VE GOT A ROBE (1927).** *See* **SPIRITUALS TRIUMPHANT OLD AND NEW,** no. 22

**50**  **JOSHUA (1927).** *See* **THIRTY AFRO-AMERICAN CHORAL SPIRITUALS,** no. 15

**51**  **JULIUS SEES HER IN ROME, GEORGIA (1935; rev. 1975)**
Musical Comedy for chorus, soloists, and orchestra
2 Acts

>    *Text:*
>>       Based on a book by Edward Boatner

*Unpublished* (LC)
*Duration:*
    2 hours
*Note:*
    Story of Julius Caesar made into a musical

**52**  **LET ME RIDE (1927).** *See* **SPIRITUALS TRIUMPHANT OLD AND NEW,** no. 23

**53**  **LET THE WORDS (1927).** *See* **SPIRITUALS TRIUMPHANT OLD AND NEW,** no. 24

  *Note:*
      A religious response, not a spiritual

**54**  **LET US BREAK BREAD TOGETHER (1944).** *See* **THIRTY AFRO-AMERICAN CHORAL SPIRITUALS,** no. 19

**LIFE OF CHRIST.** *See* **THE MAN FROM NAZARETH**

**55**  **LISTEN TO THE LAMBS (1927).** *See* **SPIRITUALS TRIUMPHANT OLD AND NEW,** no. 25

**56**  **A LITTLE TALK WITH JESUS (1927).** *See* **SPIRITUALS TRIUMPHANT OLD AND NEW,** no. 26

**57a**  **LORD, I CAN'T STAY AWAY (1944)**
For chorus (SATB), unaccompanied

  *Text:*
      Spiritual
  *Dedication:*
      To Fred Waring
  *Publication:*
      New York: Hammond Music, 1952 (IU)

**57b**  **LORD, I CAN'T STAY AWAY (1944).** *See* **THE STORY OF THE SPIRITUALS,** no. 17

**58**  **LORD, I WANT TO BE A CHRISTIAN (1927).** *See* **SPIRITUALS TRIUMPHANT OLD AND NEW,** no. 27

**59a**  **LOST SHEEP (1944).** *See* **THIRTY AFRO-AMERICAN CHORAL SPIRITUALS,** no. 14

**59b**  **LOST SHEEP (1944).** *See* **THE STORY OF THE SPIRITUALS,** no. 18

**60**  **THE MAN FROM NAZARETH (1967)**
For chorus (SATB), solo voices, narrator, and dancers

>*Text:*
>>Spiritual
>
>*Unpublished*
>*First performance:*
>>October 28, 1971; New York City; St. John the Divine Cathedral
>
>*Notes:*
>>A rock opera consisting of 25 spirituals which chronologically tell the story of Jesus.
>>Originally titled *The Life of Christ.*

**61**  **MY GOD IS SO HIGH (1927).** *See* **THIRTY AFRO-AMERICAN CHORAL SPIRITUALS,** no. 8

**62**  **MY GOOD LORD'S BEEN HERE (1927).** *See* **SPIRITUALS TRIUMPHANT OLD AND NEW,** no. 28

**63**  **MY LORD, WHAT A MOURNING (1927).** *See* **SPIRITUALS TRIUMPHANT OLD AND NEW,** no. 29

**64**  **MY TIME IS COME (1927).** *See* **THIRTY AFRO-AMERICAN CHORAL SPIRITUALS,** no. 21

**65a**  **NEW BORN (1944).** *See* **THIRTY AFRO-AMERICAN CHORAL SPIRITUALS,** no. 30

**65b** NEW BORN (1944). *See* **THE STORY OF THE SPIRITUALS**, no. 19

**66** NOBODY KNOWS THE TROUBLE I'VE SEEN (1944). *See* **THE STORY OF THE SPIRITUALS**, no. 20

**67** NOW IS THE NEEDY TIME (1927). *See* **SPIRITUALS TRIUMPHANT OLD AND NEW**, no. 30

**68** O LORD, I DONE DONE (1924)
For voice and piano

> *Text:*
>> Spiritual
> *Publication:*
>> Boston: Ditson, 1925 (HU; IU)

**69a** OH, WHAT A BEAUTIFUL CITY (1940). *See also* **THIRTY AFRO-AMERICAN CHORAL SPIRITUALS**, no. 9

> *Publication:*
>> New York: G. Schirmer, 1942

**69b** OH, WHAT A BEAUTIFUL CITY (1940)
For voice and piano

> *Publications:*
>> New York: G. Schirmer, 1940 (HU; IU).
>> New York: G. Schirmer, 1948; in: Rupp, Franz, ed. *Marian Anderson Album of Songs and Spirituals* (LC).

**70a** ON MA JOURNEY (1922). *See also* **THIRTY AFRO-AMERICAN CHORAL SPIRITUALS**, no. 12

> *Publication:*
>> New York: Ricordi, 1956 (HU; IU)

**70b**  **ON MA JOURNEY (1923)**
For voice and piano

> *Dedication:*
>> To Roland Hayes
>
> *Publication:*
>> New York: Ricordi, 1928 (HU; IU; LC; NYPL)

**71**  **PLENTY GOOD ROOM (1927).** *See also* **THE STORY OF THE SPIRITUALS,** no. 21; **SIXTEEN SOLO SPIRITUALS FOR VOICE AND PIANO,** no. 3

> *Publication:*
>> New York: Hammond Music, 1944

**72a**  **RIDE ON, KING JESUS (1944)**
For chorus (SATB), unaccompanied

> *Text:*
>> Spiritual
>
> *Dedication:*
>> To Robert Nolan
>
> *Publication:*
>> New York: Colombo, 1952 (IU)

**72b**  **RIDE ON, KING JESUS (1944).** *See* **THE STORY OF THE SPIRITUALS,** no. 22; **SIXTEEN SOLO SPIRITUALS FOR VOICE AND PIANO,** no. 7

**73a**  **RISE AND SHINE (1927).** *See* **THIRTY AFRO-AMERICAN CHORAL SPIRITUALS,** no. 26

**73b**  **RISE AND SHINE (1944).** *See* **THE STORY OF THE SPIRITUALS,** no. 23; **SIXTEEN SOLO SPIRITUALS FOR VOICE AND PIANO,** no. 13

**74**  **RISE UP SHEPHERDS AND FOLLOW.** *See* **THIRTY AFRO-AMERICAN CHORAL SPIRITUALS,** no. 29

**75**  **ROOM ENOUGH (1927).** *See* **SPIRITUALS TRIUMPHANT OLD AND NEW,** no. 31

**76**   SEE THE FOUR AND TWENTY ELDERS (1927). *See* THIRTY AFRO-AMERICAN CHORAL SPIRITUALS, no. 4

**77**   SINNER, DON'T LET THIS HARVEST PASS (1927)
For chorus (SATB), unaccompanied

> *Text:*
>> Spiritual
> *Dedication:*
>> To the Robert Shaw Choir
> *Publication:*
>> New York: Hammond Music, 1952 (IU)

**78**   SIT DOWN SERVANT (1927). *See* SPIRITUALS TRIUMPHANT OLD AND NEW, no. 32

SIXTEEN SOLO SPIRITUALS FOR VOICE AND PIANO. *See* SOLO SPIRITUALS FOR VOICE AND PIANO, SIXTEEN

SOLO SPIRITUALS FOR VOICE AND PIANO, SIXTEEN

> *Publication:*
>> New York: Hammond Music, 1964 (AU; LC)
> *Contents:*
>> 1. Done Made My Vow
>> 2. Ain't That Good News
>> 3. Plenty Good Room
>> 4. When I Get Home
>> 5. By and By
>> 6. City Called Heaven
>> 7. Ride On King Jesus
>> 8. (I) Ain't Got Weary Yet
>> 9. Steal Away
>> 10. You Hear the Lambs
>> 11. Swing Low
>> 12. Crucifixion
>> 13. Rise and Shine
>> 14. I Know the Lord
>> 15. Go Tell It on the Mountain
>> 16. They Led My Lord Away

**79a** **SOON I WILL BE DONE (1927)**
For chorus (SATB), unaccompanied

> *Text:*
>> Spiritual
>
> *Dedication:*
>> To John W. Work
>
> *Publication:*
>> New York: Ricordi, 1954 (HU; IU; LC)

**79b** **SOON I WILL BE DONE (1927)**
For voice and piano

> *Dedication:*
>> To Felix Deyo
>
> *Publication:*
>> New York: Ricordi, 1949 (IU; LC)

## SPIRITUALS TRIUMPHANT OLD AND NEW
For chorus (SATB), unaccompanied and with piano

> *Publication:*
>> Nashville, Tennessee: Sunday School Publishing Board, National
>> Baptist Convention, 1927 (AU; LC)
>
> *Contents:*
>> 1. Ain't You Glad
>> 2. All o' My Sins
>> 3. Balm in Gilead
>> 4. Can I Ride?
>> 5. Certainly Lord
>> 6. Children, Don't Get Weary
>> 7. Couldn't Hear Nobody Pray
>> 8. Crucifixion
>> 9. Down By the Riverside
>> 10. Give Me Your Hand
>> 11. Glory, Glory Hallelujah
>> 12. God's Going to Set This World on Fire
>> 13. Good News
>> 14. He's Got the Whole World in His Hands
>> 15. How Did You Feel?
>> 16. Hush! Hush!
>> 17. I Know the Lord (Laid His Hands on Me)

18. I Shall Not Be Moved
19. I'm a Soldier
20. I'm So Glad
21. In My Father's House
22. I've Got a Robe
23. Let Me Ride
24. Let the Words
25. Listen to the Lambs
26. A Little Talk With Jesus
27. Lord, I Want to Be a Christian
28. My Good Lord's Been Here
29. My Lord, What a Mourning
30. Now Is the Needy Time
31. Room Enough
32. Sit Down, Servant
33. Steal Away
34. Swing Low, Sweet Chariot
35. There is Joy in That Land
36. The Time Ain't Long
37. When the Saints Go Marching In
38. You Must Have That True Religion

**80**  **THE STAR (1944)**
For chorus (SATB), unaccompanied

>*Text:*
>>Spiritual
>*Publication:*
>>New York: Colombo, 1964 (IU; LC; HU)

**81a**  **STEAL AWAY (1927).** *See* **SPIRITUALS TRIUMPHANT OLD AND NEW,** no. 33

**81b**  **STEAL AWAY (1944).** *See* **THE STORY OF THE SPIRITUALS,** no. 24; **SIXTEEN SOLO SPIRITUALS FOR VOICE AND PIANO,** no. 9

**THE STORY OF THE SPIRITUALS; THIRTY SPIRITUALS AND THEIR ORIGINS**
For voice and piano

>*Text:*
>>Spiritual

*Dedication:*
>   To Ella Bell Davis, Abbie Mitchell, Hazel Harrison, and Hall Johnson

*Publication:*
>   New York: McAfee, 1973

*Contents:*
>   1. Ain't That Good News
>   2. Baby Bethlehem
>   3. Bye and Bye
>   4. City Called Heaven
>   5. The Crucifixion
>   6. Didn't My Lord Deliver Daniel
>   7. Done Made My Vow
>   8. Give Me Jesus
>   9. Give Me Your Hand
>   10. Go Down Moses
>   11. Go Tell It on the Mountain
>   12. He's Got the Whole World in His Hands
>   13. His Name So Sweet
>   14. I Ain't Got Weary Yet
>   15. I Know the Lord Laid His Hands on Me
>   16. I'm Troubled in Mind
>   17. Lord, I Can't Stay Away
>   18. Lost Sheep
>   19. New Born
>   20. Nobody Knows the Trouble I've Seen
>   21. Plenty Good Room
>   22. Ride On, King Jesus
>   23. Rise and Shine
>   24. Steal Away
>   25. Swing Low, Sweet Chariot
>   26. They Led My Lord Away
>   27. Wade in the Water
>   28. What You Goin' to Name the Baby
>   29. When I Get Home
>   30. You Hear the Lambs A-Crying

**82a**  **SWING LOW, SWEET CHARIOT (1927).** *See* **THIRTY AFRO-AMERICAN CHORAL SPIRITUALS,** no. 10; **SPIRITUALS TRIUMPHANT OLD AND NEW,** no. 34

**82b**  **SWING LOW, SWEET CHARIOT (1944).** *See* **THE STORY OF THE SPIRITUALS,** no. 25; **SIXTEEN SOLO SPIRITUALS FOR VOICE AND PIANO,** no. 11

83 **THAT GETTIN' UP MORNIN' (1927).** *See* **THIRTY AFRO-AMERICAN CHORAL SPIRITUALS,** no. 16

84 **THERE IS JOY IN THAT LAND (1927).** *See* **SPIRITUALS TRIUMPHANT OLD AND NEW,** no. 35

85a **THEY LED MY LORD AWAY (1944).** *See* **THIRTY AFRO-AMERICAN CHORAL SPIRITUALS,** no. 22

85b **THEY LED MY LORD AWAY (1944).** *See* **THE STORY OF THE SPIRITUALS,** no. 26; **SIXTEEN SOLO SPIRITUALS FOR VOICE AND PIANO,** no. 16

**THIRTY AFRO-AMERICAN CHORAL SPIRITUALS.** *See* **AFRO-AMERICAN CHORAL SPIRITUALS, THIRTY**

86 **THE TIME AIN'T LONG (1927).** *See* **SPIRITUALS TRIUMPHANT OLD AND NEW,** no. 36

87a **TRAMPIN' (1926)**
For chorus (SATB), unaccompanied

> *Text:*
> > Spiritual
> *Publication:*
> > New York: Galaxy, 1954 (LC; HU)

87b **TRAMPIN' (1918)**
For voice and piano

> *Publication:*
> > New York: Galaxy, 1931 (HU; IU)
> *Recording:*
> > RCA Victor LSC-2592 (1962)

88 **TROUBLED IN MIND (1975-1978)**
Opera
3 Acts

*Text:*
> By Edward Boatner

*Duration:*
> 2 1/2 hours

*Unpublished*

*Scheduled for presentation 1979-80*

*Notes:*
> Slave opera about love between a black girl and her slave owner.
> Funded by the National Endowment for the Arts.

**89  WADE IN THE WATER (1925).** *See also* **THE STORY OF THE SPIRITUALS,** no. 27

> *Publication:*
> > Boston: Ditson, 1925 (HU). *See also* Fisher, William Arms
> > *Seventy Negro Spirituals,* New York: Ditson, 1926 (IU)

**90  WERE YOU THERE? (1927).** *See also* **THIRTY AFRO-AMERICAN CHORAL SPIRITUALS,** no. 25

> *Publication:*
> New York: Hammond Music, 1952 (IU)

**91  WHAT A SHAME (1927)**
For chorus (SATB), unaccompanied

> *Text:*
> > Spiritual
> *Publication:*
> > New York: Hammond Music, 1953 (IU)

**92  WHAT YOU GOIN' TO NAME THE BABY? (1944).** *See* **THE STORY OF THE SPIRITUALS,** no. 28

**93a  WHEN I GET HOME (1944)**
For chorus (SATB), unaccompanied

> *Text:*
> > Spiritual
> *Publication:*
> > New York: Ricordi, 1954 (IU; LC)

**93b** **WHEN I GET HOME (1944).** *See* **THE STORY OF THE SPIRITUALS,** no. 29; **SIXTEEN SOLO SPIRITUALS FOR VOICE AND PIANO,** no. 4

**94** **WHEN THE SAINTS GO MARCHING IN (1916).** *See* **SPIRITUALS TRIUMPHANT OLD AND NEW,** no. 37

> *Note:*
>> Original melody by composer

**95** **WHO IS THAT YONDER? (1944)**
For chorus (SATB), unaccompanied

> *Text:*
>> Spiritual
> *Dedication:*
>> To Warner Lawson
> *Publication:*
>> New York: Colombo, 1954 (IU; LC; HU)

**96** **YOU GOT TO REAP (1927).** *See* **THIRTY AFRO-AMERICAN CHORAL SPIRITUALS,** no. 6

**97a** **YOU HEAR THE LAMBS A-CRYING (1944)**
For chorus (SATB), unaccompanied

> *Text:*
>> Spiritual
> *Publication:*
>> New York: Hammond Music, 1952 (IU)

**97b** **YOU HEAR THE LAMBS A-CRYING (1944).** *See* **THE STORY OF THE SPIRITUALS,** no. 30; **SIXTEEN SOLO SPIRITUALS FOR VOICE AND PIANO,** no. 10

**98** **YOU MUST HAVE THAT TRUE RELIGION (1927).** *See* **SPIRITUALS TRIUMPHANT OLD AND NEW,** no. 38

*Margaret Bonds, 1965*

## MARGARET ALLISON BONDS
b. Chicago, Illinois, March 3, 1913; d. Los Angeles, California, April 26, 1972

Bonds was one of the best known and most respected figures in Black music circles. She was a student at the Chicago Musical College, the Juilliard School of Music, and Northwestern University, which awarded her both the Bachelor and Master's degrees in music by the time she was twenty-one years of age. She studied with Roy Harris, Emerson Harper, Robert Starer, Florence Price, Walter Gossett, William Dawson, Carl Beecher, and other major musicians.

In 1933 she was piano soloist at the Chicago World's Fair and played with the Chicago Symphony Orchestra, marking the first appearance of a Black soloist with the orchestra. On February 7, 1952 she gave her New York piano debut in Town Hall. She later toured as a soloist and as part of a duo piano team. Her performance in 1950 with the Scranton Philharmonic was the first time a Black pianist appeared with this orchestra.

Many civic and cultural organizations benefitted from her role as music director: Stage of Youth, East Side Settlement House, White Barn Theatre, American Theater Wing, and Inner City Repertory Theater in Los Angeles. Included in her large compositional output are the background scores for three stage works: *Shakespeare in Harlem, U. S.A.,* and *Romey and Julie.* At the Inner City Institute she taught piano and theory. She was also an active member of the National Association of Negro Musicians for which she served as chairperson for the Afro-American Music of the Eastern Region.

Awards, honors, and scholarships came to her from numerous sources. In 1932 she received a prize in the Wanamaker competition for her song *Sea Ghost.* Northwestern University awarded her the Alumni Award in Arts and Letters in 1967. She also received awards from Alpha Kappa Alpha, Julius Rosenwald, and Roy Harris. The National Association of Negro Musicians awarded her a scholarship and honored her at a meeting of the Golden Gate Branch in 1971.

Leontyne Price commissioned Bonds to arrange a group of spirituals which the opera star sang in concert and for recordings. Bonds also arranged spirituals for the Los Angeles Jubilee Singers. In addition, she contributed literary articles about Black music to various reference works and journals. She was a member of ASCAP.

*Sources:*

 An

 ASCAP 1966

 "Black Composers and Their Piano Music," in *American Music
  Teacher,* February/March 1970, p. 24

 "Black Women of Achievement," in *The Black American
  Reference Book,* New Jersey: Prentice-Hall, 1976

 Cl

 Green, Mildred Denby. *A Study of the Lives and Works of Five
  Black Women Composers in America,* dissertation, University
  of Oklahoma, 1975

 Harris, Carl G., Jr. "Three Schools of Black Choral Composers
  and Arrangers," in *Choral Journal,* April 1974, vol. 14, no. 8,
  pp. 11-18

 *Musical America,* February 1952, vol. 72, p. 218

 NYB, 1952

 Wh

 Wi

# WORKS

*All unpublished works are available from Ms. Djane Richardson*
*See Introduction, page 8, footnote 1*

**1   AFRICAN DANCE**
For vocal duet

> *Text:*
>> By Langston Hughes
>
> *Unpublished*
> *First performance:*
>> By Adele Addison and Lawrence Winters


**2   AVAILABLE JONES**
For voice and piano

> *Text:*
>> By Ted Persons and Russ Smith
>
> *Unpublished*


**3   THE BALLAD OF THE BROWN KING**
Christmas Cantata for chorus (SATB), solo voices, and piano

> *Text:*
>> By Langston Hughes
>
> *Publication:*
>> New York: Sam Fox, 1961 (AU; HU; IU; LC)
>
> *Contents:*
>> 1. Of the Three Wise Men
>> 2. They Brought Fine Gifts
>> 3. Sing Alleluia
>> 4. Mary Had a Little Baby
>> 5. Now When Jesus Was Born
>> 6. Could He Have Been an Ethiope?
>> 7. Oh, Sing of the King Who Was Tall and Brown
>> 8. That Was a Christmas Long Ago
>> 9. Alleluia
>
> *First performance:*
>> December 12, 1954; New York City; Eastside Settlement House;
>>> McClain Chorale; George McClain, conductor
>
> *Notes:*
>> Originally scored for orchestra.
>> Analysis in: Green, Mildred Denby. *A Study of the Lives*
>>> *and Works of Five Black Women Composers in America.*
>> Dissertation, University of Oklahoma, 1975.
>> No. 4 published separately in choral and solo voice versions.

**4    BEYOND THE END OF THE TRAIL**
For voice and piano

> *Text:*
>> By Roger Chaney
>> *Unpublished*

**5    BIRTH**
For voice and piano

> *Text:*
>> By Langston Hughes
>> *Unpublished*

**6    BOUND (1950's)**
For voice and piano

> *Text:*
>> By Margaret Bonds
> *Dedication:*
>> "to my Larry"
>> *Unpublished*

**7    BRIGHT STAR**
For voice and piano

> *Text:*
>> By Janice Lovoos
> *Publication:*
>> Sherman Oaks, California: Solo Music, 1968
> *Note:*
>> A Christmas song

**8    CHILDREN'S SLEEP**
For chorus (SATB) and piano

> *Text:*
>> By Vernon Glasser
> *Publication:*
>> New York: Carl Fischer
> *Note:*
>> Originally written as a solo in the children's operetta, *Winter Night's Dream*

**9   CLANDESTINE ON THE MORNING LINE**
For piano
Incidental music for a stage play

>*Text:*
>>By Josh Greenfield
>*Unpublished*
>*First performance:*
>>October 1961; New York City

**10   CREDO**
For chorus (SATB), baritone solo, and orchestra

>*Text:*
>>By W. E. B. DuBois
>*Unpublished*
>*Contents:*
>>1. I Believe in the Devil and His Angels
>>2. I Believe in Liberty
>>3. I Believe in Patience
>*First performance:*
>>May 1972; Los Angeles, California; Los Angeles Philharmonic;
>>Zubin Mehta, conductor

**11   CUE 10**

>*Text:*
>>By Langston Hughes
>*Unpublished (c. 1960)*
>*Note:*
>>Alternate title: *Down and Out*

**12   DIARY OF A DIVORCEE**
For voice and piano

>*Text:*
>>By Janice Lovoos
>*Unpublished (c. 1968)*

**13   DIDN'T IT RAIN**
For voice and piano

>*Text:*
>>Spiritual
>*Publication:*
>>Bryn Mawr, Pennsylvania: Mercury, 1967 (IU)

**14  DON'T SPEAK**
For voice and piano

> *Text:*
>> By Janice Lovoos
>> *Unpublished (c. 1968)*
>> *Recorded:*
>> By Peggy Lee

**15  DOWN SOUTH IN DIXIE**
For voice and piano

> *Unpublished (c. 1933)*

**16  DREAM PORTRAITS, THREE**
For voice and piano

> *Text:*
>> By Langston Hughes from "The Dream Keeper"
> *Publication:*
>> New York: Ricordi, 1959 (AU; LC; NYPL). *See also* Patterson,
>> Willis C. *Anthology of Art Songs by Black American Composers,*
>> New York: Marks, 1971
> *Contents:*
>> 1. Dream Variations
>> 2. I, Too
>> 3. Minstrel Man
> *First performance:*
>> May 2, 1959; Columbus, Ohio; NANM concert, East High School;
>> Laurence Watson, tenor
> *Notes:*
>> No. 1 written for Adele Addison; Nos. 2,3 written for Lawrence
>> Winters.
>> Analysis in: Green, Mildred Denby. *A Study of the Lives and
>> Works of Five Black Women Composers in America.*
>> Dissertation, University of Oklahoma, 1975.

**17  DRY BONES.** *See* **FIVE SPIRITUALS**

**18  EMPTY INTERLUDE**
For voice and piano

> *Text:*
>> By Roger Chaney and Andy Razaf
> *Unpublished (c. 1941)*

**19**  **EZEKIEL SAW THE WHEEL**
For voice and piano

> *Text:*
>> Spiritual
>
> *Dedication:*
>> To Betty Allen
>
> *Publication:*
>> New York: Mercury, 1959 (AU; IU; LC); arranged for orchestra in
>> 1968; orchestra material available from Presser (New York) (HU)

**20**  **FATE IS A FUNNY THING**
For voice and piano

> *Text:*
>> By Roger Chaney and Ted Persons
>
> *Unpublished*

**21**  **FIELDS OF WONDER**
Cycle for Men's Chorus and piano (also for voice and piano)

> *Text:*
>> By Langston Hughes
>
> *Unpublished*
>
> *Contents:*
>> 1. Heaven
>> 2. Snake
>> 3. Snail
>> 4. Big Sur
>> 5. Moonlight Night
>> 6. Carmel
>> 7. New Moon
>
> *First performance:*
>> February 1964; Brooklyn, New York; Brooklyn Museum; Lincoln
>> University Glee Club

**FIVE SPIRITUALS.** *See* **SPIRITUALS, FIVE**

**22**  **FOOTPRINTS ON MY HEART**
For voice and piano

> *Text:*
>> By Marjorie May
>
> *Unpublished*

**23  GEORGIA**
For voice and piano or orchestra

> *Text:*
>> By Andy Razaf, Margaret Bonds, and Joe Davis
>
> *Unpublished (c. 1939)*
> *Notes:*
>> Co-composed with Andy Razaf and Joe Davis.
>> Also arranged as a fox trot for orchestra (c. 1939), not by Bonds.

**24  GO TELL IT ON THE MOUNTAIN**
For chorus (SATB) and piano (also for voice and piano)

> *Text:*
>> Spiritual
>
> *Publication:*
>> Bryn Mawr, Pennsylvania: Mercury, 1962 (IU)

**25  HE'S GOT THE WHOLE WORLD IN HIS HANDS**
For voice and piano

> *Text:*
>> Spiritual
>
> *Publication:*
>> Bryn Mawr, Pennsylvania: Mercury, 1963
>
> *Recording:*
>> RCA Victor LM/LSC 2600 (1962)
>
> *Note:*
>> Arranged for Leontyne Price

**26a  HOLD ON**
For voice and piano

> *Text:*
>> Spiritual
>
> *Publication:*
>> Bryn Mawr, Pennsylvania: Mercury, 1962 (IU)

**26b  HOLD ON**
For chorus (SATB) and orchestra

> *Publication:*
> New York: Presser, 1968

**27  I GOT A HOME IN THAT ROCK**
For voice (medium) and piano

> *Text:*
>> Spiritual
>
> *Commission and dedication:*
>> To Betty Allen
>
> *Publication:*
>> Bryn Mawr, Pennsylvania: Mercury, 1968 (IU); orchestral material available from Presser, New York
>
> *Note:*
>> Analysis in: Green, Mildred Denby. *A Study of the Lives and Works of Five Black Women Composers in America.* Dissertation, University of Oklahoma, 1975

**28  I SHALL PASS THROUGH THIS WORLD**
For chorus (SATB), unaccompanied

> *Text:*
>> By Etienne De Grellet
>
> *Publication:*
>> New York: Bourne, 1967 (HU; IU)

**29  I WANT JESUS TO WALK WITH ME**
Spiritual for cello and piano

> *Unpublished*
> *First performance:*
>> September 10, 1964; Maryland; Kermit Moore, cello

**30  I WISH I KNEW HOW IT WOULD FEEL TO BE FREE**
For voice, chorus, and orchestra

> *Text:*
>> Spiritual
>
> *Unpublished*
> *Recording:*
>> RCA Victor LSC-3183
>
> *Note:*
>> Arranged for Leontyne Price

**31** **IF YOU'RE NOT THERE (1939)**
For chorus (SATB) and piano

> *Text:*
>> By Andy Razaf
>> *Unpublished*

**32** **I'LL REACH TO HEAVEN.** *See* **FIVE SPIRITUALS**

**33** **I'M GOING TO RENO**
For voice and piano

> *Unpublished (c. 1935)*
> *Note:*
>> A "fox trot song"

**34** **I'M GONNA DO A SONG AND A DANCE**
For chorus (unison) and piano

> *Text:*
>> By Bill Cairo
>> *Unpublished*

**35** **I'M SO IN LOVE**
Melody line only

> *Text:*
>> By Margaret Bonds and Leonard Reed
>> *Unpublished (c. 1937)*
>> *Note:*
>>> Co-composed with Leonard Reed

**36** **JOSHUA FIT DA BATTLE OF JERICHO**
For voice (medium) and piano or orchestra

> *Text:*
>> Spiritual
> *Publication:*
>> Bryn Mawr, Pennsylvania: Mercury, 1967 (piano) (IU); orchestral
>> material available from Presser, New York

**37    JOY (1954)**
For chorus (SAT), string quartet, and piano

> *Text:*
>> By Langston Hughes
>
> *Unpublished*
> *First performance:*
>> By McClain Chorale; George McClain, conductor

**38    LADY BY THE MOON I VOW**
For voice and piano

> *Text:*
>> By Robert Dunmore
>
> *Unpublished (c. 1936)*

**39    LET'S MAKE A DREAM COME TRUE**
For voice and piano

> *Text:*
>> By Roger Chaney
>
> *Unpublished*

**40    LET'S MEET TONIGHT IN A DREAM**
For voice and piano

> *Text:*
>> By Roger Chaney
>
> *Unpublished*

**41    LITTLE DAVID PLAY ON YOUR HARP**
For voice and piano

> *Text:*
>> Spiritual
>
> *Unpublished*
> *First performance:*
>> March 25, 1956; New York City; Town Hall; Laurence
>> Watson, tenor

**42    LORD, I JUST CAN'T KEEP FROM CRYIN'.** *See* **FIVE SPIRITUALS**

**43    LOVE AIN'T WHAT IT OUGHT TO BE**
For voice and piano

> *Unpublished (c. 1935)*


**44    MASS IN D MINOR**
For chorus (SATB) and organ

> *Unpublished*
> *First performance:*
>> March 15, 1959; New York City; St. Phillip's Episcopal Church


**45    MIDTOWN AFFAIR (1950's)**
Musical

> *Text:*
>> By Roger Chaney
> *Unpublished*
> *Contents:*
>> 1. You Give Me a Lift
>> 2. Mist Over Manhattan
>> 3. I Love the Lie I'm Living
>> 4. My Kind of Man


**46    THE MIGRATION**
Ballet for piano and instrumental ensemble

> *Unpublished*
> *First performance:*
>> March 7, 1964; New York City; YM-YWHA; Teresa L. Kaufman
>> Concert Hall


**47    MONTGOMERY VARIATIONS (1965)**
For orchestra

> *Dedication:*
>> To Martin Luther King, Jr.
> *Unpublished*
> *Contents:*
>> 1. Jesus Walk With Me
>> 2. Prayer Meeting
>> 3. March

4. One Sunday in the South
5. Dawn in Dixie

*Note:*

Written for the March on Montgomery, Alabama in 1965

**48    THE MOON WINKED TWICE**

For voice and piano

*Text:*

By Margaret Bonds, Dan Burley, and Dorothy Sachs

*Unpublished (c. 1941)*

*Note:*

Co-composed with Dan Burley and Dorothy Sachs

**49a    THE NEGRO SPEAKS OF RIVERS (1941)**

For voice and piano

*Text:*

By Langston Hughes

*Publication:*

In Handy, William C. *Unsung Americans Sung,* New York:
Handy Bros., 1942 (AU; HU; IU; LC)

*Notes:*

Alternate title: *I've Known Rivers.*

Analysis in: Green, Mildred Denby. *A Study of the Lives and
Works of Five Black Women Composers in America.*
Dissertation, University of Oklahoma, 1975.

**49b    THE NEGRO SPEAKS OF RIVERS**

For chorus (SATB) and piano

*Dedication:*

To Albert J. McNeil and the Sanctuary Choir

*Publication:*

New York: Handy Bros., 1962 (HU)

*First performance:*

May 25, 1941; New York City; Town Hall; Belmont Balladiers;
Fritz Weller, conductor

**50    THE NEW YORK BLUES**

For voice and piano

*Text:*

By Malone Dickerson

*Unpublished (c. 1938)*

**51**   **THE PASTURE (1958)**
For voice (soprano) and piano

> *Text:*
>> By Robert Frost
>
> *Unpublished*
> *First performance:*
>> August 9, 1959; Palo Alto, California; Stanford University;
>> Sigma Alpha Iota 29th Triennial National Convention;
>> Marjorie McClung, soprano

**52**   **PEACHTREE STREET (1939)**
For voice and piano

> *Text:*
>> By Andy Razaf, Margaret Bonds, and Joe Davis
>
> *Unpublished*
> *Recorded:*
>> By Glenn Miller, Charley Spivak, Woody Hermann,
>> and others
>
> *Notes:*
>> Co-composed with Andy Razaf and Joe Davis.
>> In "Gone With the Wind."

**53**   **PETER GO RING DEM BELLS**
For chorus and string quartet

> *Text:*
>> Spiritual
>
> *Unpublished*
> *First performance:*
>> September 9, 1956; New York City; Town Hall; Uptown
>> Men's Chorale

**54**   **POT POURRI**
For voice and piano

> *Text:*
>> By Janice Lovoos and Edmund Penney
>
> *Unpublished (c. 1968)*

**55**   **PRAISE THE LORD**
For chorus (SATB)

> *Unpublished*
> *First performance:*
>> May 16-29, 1965, Yonkers, New York; Cain choristers;
>> Alfred E. Cain, conductor

**56**   **THE PRICE OF A LOVE AFFAIR**

> *Text:*
>> By Ernest Richman
> *Unpublished (c. 1957)*

**57**   **QUINTET IN F MAJOR (1933)**
For piano quintet

> *Unpublished*
> *In one movement*

**58**   **RADIO BALLROOM**
For voice and piano

> *Text:*
>> By Andy Razaf
> *Unpublished (c. 1940)*
> *Note:*
>> Co-composed with Andy Razaf

**59**   **RAINBOW GOLD**
For voice (medium) and piano

> *Text:*
>> By Roger Chaney
> *Publication:*
>> New York: Chappell, 1956 (AU; IU)

**60**   **ROMEY AND JULIE**
Incidental music for a stage play

> *Text:*
>> By Robert Dunmore
> *Unpublished*

**61  SCRIPTURE READING**
For chamber orchestra

> *Commissioned:*
>> By Nicklauss Wyss, conductor of the Little Symphony of
>> San Francisco Symphony Orchestra
>
> *Unpublished*

**62  SEA GHOST**
For voice and piano

> *Unpublished*
> *Note:*
>> Won Wanamaker Prize 1932

**63  SHAKESPEARE IN HARLEM**
Incidental music for a stage play

> *Text:*
>> By Langston Hughes
>
> *Unpublished*

**64  SIN WEARY**
For voice, melody line only

> *Text:*
>> By Robert Dunmore
>
> *Unpublished (c. 1938)*
> *Note:*
>> From *Romey and Julie*

**65  SING AHO**
For voice (medium) and piano

> *Text:*
>> Spiritual
>
> *Dedication:*
>> To Betty Allen
>
> *Publication:*
>> New York: Chappell, 1960 (IU)

**66   THE SINGIN' MOUSE**
For voice, melody line only

> *Text:*
>> By Henry Douté
>
> *Unpublished (c. 1937)*

**67   SINNER, PLEASE DON'T LET THIS HARVEST PASS**
For voice, chorus (SATB), and orchestra

> *Text:*
>> Spiritual
>
> *Unpublished*
> *Recording:*
>> RCA Victor LSC-3183
>
> *Note:*
>> Arranged for Leontyne Price

**68   SIT DOWN SERVANT.** *See* **FIVE SPIRITUALS**

> *Recording:*
>> RCA Victor LM/LSC-2600 (1962)

**69   SONGS OF THE SEASONS**
Cycle for voice and piano

> *Text:*
>> By Langston Hughes
>
> *Commissioned:*
>> By Laurence Watson
>
> *Unpublished*
> *Contents:*
>> 1. Poeme d'Automne
>> 2. Winter Moon
>> 3. Young Love in Spring
>> 4. Summer Storm
>
> *First performance:*
>> March 25, 1956; New York City; Town Hall;
>> Laurence Watson, tenor

**70   SPIRITUAL SUITE**
For piano

> *Unpublished*

**SPIRITUALS, FIVE (1942)**
For voice (high) and orchestra

> *Text:*
>> Spiritual
>
> *Commissioned:*
>> By Hortense Love
>
> *Publication:*
>> New York: Mutual Music, 1946; orchestra parts on rental from
>> Chappell, New York
>
> *Contents:*
>> 1. Dry Bones
>> 2. Sit Down Servant
>> 3. Lord, I Just Can't Keep From Cryin'
>> 4. You Can Tell the World
>> 5. I'll Reach to Heaven
>
> *First performance:*
>> 1942; New York City; Town Hall; Hortense Love, soprano

**71    SPRING WILL BE SO SAD WHEN SHE COMES THIS YEAR (1940)**
For voice (medium) and piano

> *Text:*
>> By Margaret Bonds and Harold Dickinson
>
> *Publication:*
>> New York: Mutual Music, 1941 (IU; NYPL)
>
> *Instrumental arrangement performed:*
>> By Glenn Miller
>
> *Recorded:*
>> By Glenn Miller, Charley Spivak, Woody Hermann and others
>
> *Notes:*
>> Co-composed with Harold Dickinson.
>> Contains diagrams for guitar accompaniment.

**72    STANDIN' IN THE NEED OF PRAYER**
For voice, chorus (SATB), and orchestra

> *Text:*
>> Spiritual
>
> *Unpublished*
>
> *Recording:*
>> RCA Victor LSC-3183
>
> *Note:*
>> Arranged for Leontyne Price

**73**  **SUPPLICATION (1950's)**
For chorus (SSAATTBB) and piano

>  *Text:*
>>  By Roger Chaney
>  *Dedication:*
>>  To Harry Revel and George Marion, Jr.
>  *Unpublished*


**74**  **SWING LOW, SWEET CHARIOT**
For voice and piano

>  *Text:*
>>  Spiritual
>  *Unpublished*
>  *First performance:*
>>  May 22, 1952; New York City


**75**  **THAT SWEET SILENT LOVE**
For voice, melody line only

>  *Text:*
>>  By Langston Hughes
>  *Unpublished (c. 1937)*


**76**  **THIS LITTLE LIGHT OF MINE**
For voice, chorus (SATB), and orchestra

>  *Text:*
>>  Spiritual
>  *Unpublished*
>  *Recording:*
>>  RCA Victor LM/LSC-2600 (1962)
>  *Note:*
>>  Arranged for Leontyne Price


**THREE DREAM PORTRAITS.** *See* **DREAM PORTRAITS, THREE**


**77**  **THREE SHEEP IN A PASTURE**
For piano

>  *Unpublished (c. 1940)*

**78**  **TO A BROWN GIRL, DEAD**
For voice and piano

> *Text:*
>> By Countee Cullen
>
> *Commissioned:*
>> By Etta Moten
>
> *Publication:*
>> Boston: Row, 1956
>
> *First performance:*
>> By John Miles, tenor
>
> *Note:*
>> Analysis in: Green, Mildred Denby. *A Study of the Lives and Works of Five Black Women Composers in America.* Dissertation, University of Oklahoma, 1975

**79**  **TRAMPIN'**
For voice (high) and piano

> *Text:*
>> Spiritual
>
> *Publication:*
>> New York: Galaxy, 1931 (IU)

**80**  **TROUBLED WATER**
For piano

> *Dedication:*
>> To Toy Harper
>
> *Publication:*
>> New York: Sam Fox, 1967 (IU)
>
> *Notes:*
>> Based on the spiritual *Wade in the Water.*
>> Analysis in: "Black Composers and Their Piano Music," in *American Music Teacher,* February/March 1970, p. 24.

**81**  **U.S.A.**
Incidental music for a stage play

> *Unpublished*

**82**    **WEST COAST BLUES**
For voice

> *Unpublished (c. 1938)*


**83**    **WHEN THE DOVE ENTERS IN**
For voice and piano

>    *Text:*
>             By Langston Hughes
>    *Unpublished (c. 1963)*


**84**    **YOU CAN TELL THE WORLD.** *See* **FIVE SPIRITUALS**
Also set for chorus (TTBB), (SSA), (SATB), unaccompanied

>    *Publication:*
>             New York: Mutual Music, 1964


**85**    **YOU'RE PRETTY SPECIAL**
For voice and piano

>    *Text:*
>             By Dorothy Sachs
>    *Unpublished (c. 1941)*

*Edgar Rogie Clark*

## EDGAR ROGIE CLARK
*b. Atlanta, Georgia, April 4, 1917; d. Detroit, Michigan, February 15, 1978*


Clark obtained his undergraduate education at Clark College in Atlanta, where he
received a Bachelor of Arts degree in 1935. He continued his studies at the Juillard
School of Music, the Chicago Musical College, the Berkshire Music Center, and
Columbia University which awarded him a Master of Arts degree in 1942. At
various times he was head of the music departments at Fort Valley State College
in Georgia, Jackson State College in Jackson, Mississippi, and Central State College
in Wilberforce, Ohio. During the Second World War he was club director for the
USO Clubs. He lectured at numerous institutions including the New Lincoln
School and the New School for Social Research (both in New York City), Wayne
State University, and New Haven State College. He directed radio and television
programs and choral groups. As a singer he gave recitals and appeared in several
Broadway productions, including *Carmen Jones* and *Porgy and Bess.* A grant was
awarded to him in 1952 by the Ford Foundation for work towards an advanced
degree at Columbia University and research in Haiti; the following year he received
a fellowship from the John Hay Whitney Foundation, which allowed him to write
a book on Black music. In addition in 1974 he was the recipient of a National
Endowment of the Humanities Fellowship to "bring Black studies back to life."
The National Association of Negro Musicians honored him with an Award of Merit.
   Clark was the author of several books of plays and poems and numerous journal
articles, primarily in the field of Negro folk music, his main interest and area of
knowledge. During his childhood, he was exposed to folk songs and, later, many
trips throughout the United States, Jamaica, Haiti, and Trinidad increased his
understanding of the music of his people. He gave many lectures on this subject

*59*

and served as folk song interpreter for many institutions. In addition he edited many compilations of Negro folk songs such as *Copper Sun* (Bryn Mawr, Presser, 1957) and authored a school text, entitled *Afro-America Sings* (Detroit: Board of Education of the City of Detroit, 1971). Clark was the compiler of *Negro Art Songs* (New York: E. B. Marks, 1946; Ann Arbor, Michigan, University Microfilms) and the Afro-American Six Series (New York: E. B. Marks). A former faculty member of Wayne County Community College, Clark taught at Marygrove College and consulted for the Detroit public schools and the Warren Woods, Michigan Board of Education. He was the founder of the International Council of Negro Folklore and was a member of ASCAP, American Folklore Society, Phi Mu Alpha Sinfonia, National Association of Teachers of Singing, African-American Institute, and others.

*Sources:*

Information submitted by composer
An
Clark, E. R., compiler *Negro Art Songs,* New York: Marks, 1946
Lawless, Ray M. *Folksingers and Folksongs in America*, New York: Duell, Sloan, Pearce, 1965
NYB 1941-1947, 1952
To
Wh
Who-C 1941-1947

## AFRICAN SONGS, SIX (1975)
For chorus (SATB), unaccompanied

> *Text:*
>> Negro folk
>
> *Publication:*
>> New York: E. B. Marks, 1975
>
> *Contents:*
>> 1. Hey, Motswala
>> 2. Kaffir Drinking Dance Song
>> 3. Everybody Loves Saturday Night
>> 4. The Proverbs
>> 5. The Hare's Dance Song
>> 6. Song of Farewell

## AFRO-AMERICAN CAROLS FOR CHRISTMAS, SIX (1971)
For chorus (SATB), unaccompanied

> *Text:*
>> Negro folk
>
> *Publication:*
>> New York: E. B. Marks, 1971 (HU; IU)
>
> *Contents:*
>> 1. Christ is Born
>> 2. Creole Christmas Carol
>> 3. Go Tell It On the Mountain
>> 4. Mary Had a Baby
>> 5. The New-Born Babe
>> 6. Rise Up, Shepherd

## AFRO-AMERICAN CAROLS FOR CHRISTMAS, SIX MORE (1973)
For chorus (SATB), unaccompanied

> *Text:*
>> Negro folk
>
> *Publication:*
>> New York: E. B. Marks, 1973 (HU)
>
> *Contents:*
>> 1. Sister Mary
>> 2. O Mary
>> 3. Sing Christ is Born
>> 4. Song of Judea
>> 5. Go Where I Send Thee
>> 6. Angels, Ring Them Bells

**AFRO-AMERICAN CAROLS FOR EASTER, SIX (1971)**
For chorus (SATB), unaccompanied

> *Text:*
>> Negro folk
> *Publication:*
>> New York: E. B. Marks, 1971 (HU)
> *Contents:*
>> 1. Calvary
>> 2. The Crucifixion
>> 3. He Rose From the Dead
>> 4. One Sunday Morning
>> 5. They Led My Lord Away
>> 6. Were You There?

1  **AMERICA 1976 (1975)**
For chorus (SATB) and piano

> *Text:*
>> Based on the Smith/Carey text
> *Unpublished*
> *Duration:*
>> 10 minutes

2  **ANGELS, RING THEM BELLS.** *See* **SIX MORE AFRO-AMERICAN CAROLS FOR CHRISTMAS**

3  **THE BAMBOULA (1956)**
For 2 pianos

> *Unpublished*
> *Duration:*
>> 6 minutes
> *First performance:*
>> 1956; Jackson, Mississippi; Jackson State College
> *Note:*
>> Based on the arrangement by Coleridge-Taylor

4  **CALVARY.** *See* **SIX AFRO-AMERICAN CAROLS FOR EASTER**

**5   CANTATE BACHINEGRAS (1974)**
For chorus (SATB), soprano, tenor, and baritone solos and piano or organ

> *Text:*
> > Spiritual
> *Unpublished*
> *Duration:*
> > 1 hour
> *Note:*
> > Traditional spirituals and arias in the style of J. S. Bach

**6   CHRIST IS BORN.** *See* **SIX AFRO-AMERICAN CAROLS FOR CHRISTMAS**

**7   COME, LITTLE DONKEY.** *See* **COPPER SUN**

**COPPER SUN (1957)**
For voice (mezzo-soprano) and piano

> *Text:*
> > Negro folk
> *Publication:*
> > Bryn Mawr, Pennsylvania: Presser, 1957 (IU)
> *Contents:*
> > 1. Steel Got to be Drove
> > 2. Nine Foot Shovel
> > 3. Upon de Mountain
> > 4. Told My Cap'n
> > 5. John Henry (the contest)
> > 6. John Henry (his death)
> > 7. The Ol' Ark's A-Moverin'
> > 8. Sit Down, Servant, Sit Down
> > 9. Take Yo' Time
> > 10. Come, Little Donkey
> > 11. Swing Along, Sue
> > 12. Hush, Li'l Baby
> > 13. Musieu Banjo
> > 14. Feel So Sad and Sorrowful
> > 15. Midnight Train
> > 16. Koliko

8   CREOLE CHRISTMAS CAROL. *See* **SIX AFRO-AMERICAN CAROLS FOR CHRISTMAS**


9   THE CRUCIFIXION. *See* **SIX AFRO-AMERICAN CAROLS FOR EASTER**


10   **DIVERTIMENTO (1969)**
For string quartet

> *Unpublished*
> *Duration:*
>> 13 minutes
> *First performance:*
>> 1970 in Detroit


11   **EARTH-CHANT (1973)**
For chorus (SATB), baritone solo with piano

> *Unpublished*
> *Duration:*
>> 7 minutes
> *First performance:*
>> March 23, 1973; Detroit, Michigan; Northwestern High School
>> Concert Choir
> *Note:*
>> Dramtic work


12   **ELEGIA (1968)**
For string orchestra

> *Dedication:*
>> To the memory of Martin Luther King
> *Unpublished*
> *Duration:*
>> 10 minutes
> *First performance:*
>> 1970; Detroit, Michigan; Detroit Metropolitan Orchestra;
>> Charles Sumner, conductor

**13**  **ETUDE (1974)**
For violin and piano

> *Unpublished*
> *Duration:*
>> 10 minutes
> *First performance:*
>> 1976; Detroit, Michigan; Joseph Striplin, violin; Detroit
>> Symphony Orchestra

**14**  **EVERYBODY LOVES SATURDAY NIGHT.** *See* **SIX AFRICIAN SONGS**

**15**  **FANTASIA (1968)**
For clarinet and piano

> *Unpublished*
> *Duration:*
>> 20 minutes
> *Three movements*
> *First performance:*
>> 1968

**16**  **FEEL SO SAD AND SORROWFUL.** *See* **COPPER SUN**

**17**  **FETE CREOLE (1970)**
For orchestra

> *Unpublished*
> *Duration:*
>> 8 minutes
> *First performance:*
>> October 27, 1970; Detroit, Michigan; Community Arts Auditorium;
>> Detroit Metropolitan Orchestra; Charles Sumner, conductor
> *Note:*
>> Based on Creole themes

**18**  **FIGURINE (1965)**
For cello and piano

> *Unpublished*
> *Duration:*
>> 15 minutes

**19    GLORY TO THE NEWBORN KING (1962)**
For chorus (SATB) and piano

> *Text:*
>> Spiritual
> *Unpublished*
> *Duration:*
>> 5 minutes
> *First performance:*
>> 1965; Detroit, Michigan; Central High School

**20    GO DOWN MOSES (1952)**
For chorus (SATB), unaccompanied

> *Text:*
>> Spiritual
> *Publication:*
>> New York: Bourne, 1953 (LC)

**21    GO TELL IT ON THE MOUNTAIN.** *See* **SIX AFRO-AMERICAN CAROLS FOR CHRISTMAS**

**22    GO WHERE I SEND THEE.** *See* **SIX MORE AFRO-AMERICAN CAROLS FOR CHRISTMAS**

**23    GWINE UP (1941)**
For chorus (SATB), unaccompanied

> *Text:*
>> Spiritual
> *Publication:*
>> Chicago: Music Products, 1941

**24    THE HARE'S DANCE SONG.** *See* **SIX AFRICAN SONGS**

**25    HE ROSE FROM THE DEAD.** *See* **SIX AFRO-AMERICAN CAROLS FOR EASTER**

**26**  HEY, MOTSWALA. *See* **SIX AFRICAN SONGS**

**27**  HILL AND GULLY. *See* **SIX WEST INDIAN SONGS**

**28**  HUSH LI'L BABY. *See* **COPPER SUN**

**29**  IMPRESSION (LE RÉVEILLON) (1946)
For voice and piano

> *Text:*
>> By Oscar Wilde
>
> *Publication:*
>> New York: E. B. Marks, 1946; in: *Negro Art Songs* (AU; LC)
>> (Reproduction available from University Microfilms,
>> Ann Arbor, Michigan)
>
> *Duration:*
>> 4 minutes

**30a**  JOHN HENRY (the contest). *See* **COPPER SUN**

**30b**  JOHN HENRY (his death). *See* **COPPER SUN**

**31**  JOHN HENRY FANTASY (1973)
For concert band

> *Unpublished*
> *Duration:*
>> 12 minutes
>
> *First performance:*
>> March 23, 1973; Detroit, Michigan; Northwestern High School
>> Band; Charles Hicks, conductor

**32**  JUBILEE (1970)
For piano

> *Unpublished*
> *Duration:*
>> 4 minutes

**33**  **KAFFIR DRINKING DANCE SONG.** *See* **SIX AFRICAN SONGS**

**34**  **KAFFIR DRINKING SONG (1976)**
For voice (baritone) and orchestra

> *Text:*
>> Traditional African
> *Unpublished*
> *Duration:*
>> 4 minutes
> *First performance:*
>> February 11, 1976; Detroit, Michigan; Willis Patterson, baritone;
>> Detroit Symphony Orchestra; Paul Freeman, conductor

**35**  **KOLIKO.** *See* **COPPER SUN**

**36**  **LARGHETTO (1970)**
For string orchestra

> *Unpublished*
> *Duration:*
>> 15 minutes

**37**  **LET US CHEER THE WEARY TRAVELER (1955)**
For chorus (SATB), unaccompanied

> *Text:*
>> Spiritual
> *Publication:*
>> New York: Boosey and Hawkes, 1955 (IU; LC; HU)

**38**  **LINSTEAD MARKET.** *See* **SIX WEST INDIAN SONGS**

**39**  **LITTLE DAVID (1971)**
For chorus (SAB) and piano

> *Text:*
>> Spiritual
> *Publication:*
>> Detroit: Detroit Board of Education, 1971; in: *Afro-America Sings* (IU)
> *Duration:*
>> 3 minutes

**40  THE LONELY ISLAND (1965)**
Ballet music for piano
> *Unpublished*
> *Duration:*
>> 1 hour 10 minutes

**41  MANGO WALK (1956)**
For chorus (SATB) and piano
> *Text:*
>> Jamaican folk
> *Publication:*
>> New York: Boosey and Hawkes, 1956 (IU; LC; HU)
> *Note:*
>> Based on a Jamaican folk tune (Rhumba)

**42  MARY HAD A BABY.** *See* **SIX AFRO-AMERICAN CAROLS FOR CHRISTMAS**

**43  MIDNIGHT TRAIN.** *See* **COPPER SUN**

**44  MISTER BANJO (1955)**
For chorus (SATB) with piano
> *Text:*
>> Negro folk
> *Publication:*
>> Chicago: Kjos, 1955 (LC)
> *Notes:*
>> Based on a Creole folk song.
>> a.k.a. *Musieu Banjo.*

**MUSIEU BANJO.** *See* **MISTER BANJO**
For chorus (SATB) with piano

**45  MUSIEU BANJO.** *See* **COPPER SUN**

**46  THE NEW-BORN BABE.** *See* **SIX AFRO-AMERICAN CAROLS FOR CHRISTMAS**

**47**  NINE FOOT SHOVEL. *See* COPPER SUN

**48**  NORTHBOUN' (1951)
For voice and piano

> *Text:*
>> By Lucy Ariel Williams
>
> *Publication:*
>> New York: E. B. Marks, 1946; in: *Negro Art Songs* (AU; LC)
>> (Reproduction available from University Microfilms,
>> Ann Arbor, Michigan)
>
> *Duration:*
>> 6 minutes

**49**  O MARY. *See* SIX MORE AFRO-AMERICAN CAROLS FOR CHRISTMAS

**50**  O, NOT A CENT. *See* SIX WEST INDIAN SONGS

**51**  THE OL' ARK'S A-MOVERIN'. *See* COPPER SUN

**52**  ONE SUNDAY MORNING. *See* SIX AFRO-AMERICAN CAROLS FOR
EASTER

**53**  PACK SHE BACK TO SHE MA. *See* SIX WEST INDIAN SONGS
Also published as single melody line; Morristown, New Jersey: Silver Burdette,
1967; in: *Music in Our Times*, p. 24 (IU)

**54**  PETER GO RING THEM BELLS (1941)
For chorus (SATB), unaccompanied

> *Text:*
>> Spiritual
>
> *Publication:*
>> Chicago: Music Products, 1941

**55  PIPPA'S SONG (1971)**
For chorus (SAB) and piano

> *Text:*
>> By Robert Browning: "Pippa Passes"
>
> *Publication:*
>> Detroit: Detroit Board of Education, 1971; in: *Afro-American Sings* (IU)


**56  PRELUDES, THREE (1970)**
For piano

> *Unpublished*
> *Duration:*
>> 12 minutes
>
> *First performance:*
>> 1972; Detroit, Michigan


**57  THE PROVERBS.** *See* **SIX AFRICAN SONGS**


**58  RIDE ON KING JESUS (1951)**
For chorus (SATB), unaccompanied

> *Text:*
>> Spiritual
>
> *Dedication:*
>> To the 75th anniversary of Jackson College
>
> *Publication:*
>> Chicago: Kjos, 1951 (LC)


**59  RISE UP, SHEPHERD.** *See* **SIX AFRO-AMERICAN CAROLS FOR CHRISTMAS**


**60  THE SERENADE (1968)**
For chorus (SATB) and piano

> *Text:*
>> By Edgar Rogie Clark
>
> *Unpublished*
> *Duration:*
>> 8 minutes

61 **SING CHRIST IS BORN.** *See* **SIX MORE AFRO-AMERICAN CAROLS FOR CHRISTMAS**

62 **SING YE GLAD PRAISES, ALLELUIA (1949)**
For chorus (SATB), unaccompanied

> *Text:*
>> Song of St. Francis
> *Publication:*
>> Glen Rock, New Jersey: J. Fischer, 1941

63 **SISTER MARY.** *See* **SIX MORE AFRO-AMERICAN CAROLS FOR CHRISTMAS**

64 **SIT DOWN SERVANT (1955)**
For chorus (SATB), soprano solo, unaccompanied

> *Text:*
>> Spiritual
> *Publication:*
>> New York: Boosey and Hawkes, 1955 (HU; IU; LC)

65 **SIT DOWN, SERVANT, SIT DOWN.** *See* **COPPER SUN**

**SIX AFRICAN SONGS.** *See* **AFRICAN SONGS, SIX**

**SIX AFRO-AMERICAN CAROLS FOR CHRISTMAS.** *See* **AFRO-AMERICAN CAROLS FOR CHRISTMAS, SIX**

**SIX AFRO-AMERICAN CAROLS FOR EASTER.** *See* **AFRO-AMERICAN CAROLS FOR EASTER, SIX**

**SIX MORE AFRO-AMERICAN CAROLS FOR CHRISTMAS.** *See* **AFRO-AMERICAN CAROLS FOR CHRISTMAS, SIX MORE**

**SIX WEST INDIAN SONGS.** *See* **WEST INDIAN SONGS, SIX**

**66**    **SONG OF FAREWELL.** *See* **SIX AFRICAN SONGS**


**67**    **SONG OF JUDEA.** *See also* **SIX MORE AFRO-AMERICAN CAROLS FOR CHRISTMAS**
For chorus (SATB)

>    *Text:*
>>    Negro folk
>    *Publication:*
>>    Delaware Water Gap, Pennsylvania: Shawnee Music, 1941 (IU)


**68**    **SONG OF THE POP BOTTLES (1965)**
For chorus (SAB) and piano

>    *Text:*
>>    By Morris Bishop "From a Bowl of Bishop"
>    *Publication:*
>>    Detroit: Detroit Board of Education, 1971; in: *Afro-America Sings* (IU)
>    *Duration:*
>>    5 minutes


**69**    **SOON-A WILL BE DONE (1951)**
For chorus (SATB), unaccompanied

>    *Text:*
>>    Spiritual
>    *Dedication:*
>>    To the 75th anniversary of Jackson College
>    *Publication:*
>>    Chicago: Kjos, 1951 (HU; LC)


**70**    **STEEL GOT TO BE DROVE.** *See* **COPPER SUN**


**71**    **THE STRANGER (1967)**
Opera for 4 characters and chamber orchestra (13 players)

>    *Text:*
>>    Based on Rupert Brooke's play
>    *Unpublished*
>    *Duration:*
>>    1 hour 45 minutes
>    *One act*

72 SWING ALONG, SUE. *See* **COPPER SUN**

73 **TAKE THIS HAMMER (1971)**
For voice and piano

> *Text:*
>> Negro folk
>
> *Publication:*
>> Detroit: Detroit Board of Education, 1971; in: *Afro-America Sings* (IU)
>
> *Note:*
>> Work song

74 **TAKE YO' TIME.** *See* **COPPER SUN**

75 **TARANTELLA (1967)**
For piano

> *Unpublished*
> *Duration:*
>> 7 minutes

76 **THERE'S A MAN GOIN' ROUN'**
For chorus (SATB), soprano solo, with piano

> *Text:*
>> Spiritual
>
> *Publication:*
>> New York: Handy Bros., 1940 (HU)

77 **THEY LED MY LORD AWAY.** *See* **SIX AFRO-AMERICAN CAROLS FOR EASTER**

78 **THIS WICKED RACE (1976)**
For voice (baritone) and orchestra

> *Text:*
>> Spiritual (adapted and arranged by composer)
>
> *Unpublished*

*Duration:*
>5 minutes

*First performance:*
>February 11, 1976; Detroit, Michigan; Willis Patterson, baritone;
>Detroit Symphony Orchestra; Paul Freeman, conductor

**THREE PRELUDES.** *See* **PRELUDES, THREE**

**79    TI YETTE (1940)**
Opera for 4 characters, chorus, and chamber orchestra

>*Text:*
>>Adapted from the play by John Matthews

>*Unpublished*
>*Duration:*
>>1 hour 20 minutes

>*First performance:*
>>June 21, 1959; Detroit, Michigan

**80    TINGA LAYO.** *See also* **SIX WEST INDIAN SONGS**

>*Publication:*
>>New York: Boosey and Hawkes, 1956 (HU; LC)

>*Note:*
>>Donkey song from Martinique

**81    TOLD MY CAP'N.** *See* **COPPER SUN**

**82    TRAMPING (1941)**
For chorus (SATB), unaccompanied

>*Text:*
>>Spiritual

>*Publication:*
>>Chicago: Music Products, 1941

>*Duration:*
>>4 minutes

**83**  UPON DE MOUNTAIN.  *See* **COPPER SUN**

**84a**  WADE IN THE WATER (1951)
For chorus (SATB), unaccompanied

> *Text:*
> > Spiritual
> *Dedication:*
> > To W. W. E. Blanchet
> *Publication:*
> > New York: E. B. Marks, 1941 (HU; IU)

**84b**  WADE IN THE WATER (1951)
For chorus (SSA), unaccompanied

> *Dedication:*
> > To Bennett College Glee Club, Greensboro, North Carolina
> *Publication:*
> > New York: E. B. Marks, 1941 (HU; IU)

**85**  WATER COME-A ME EYE.  *See* **SIX WEST INDIAN SONGS**

**86**  WERE YOU THERE?  *See* **SIX AFRO-AMERICAN CAROLS FOR EASTER**

WEST INDIAN SONGS, SIX (1976)
For chorus (SATB), unaccompanied

> *Text:*
> > Negro folk
> *Publication:*
> > New York: E. B. Marks, 1976
> *Contents:*
> > 1. Linstead Market
> > 2. O, Not a Cent
> > 3. Water Come-A Me Eye
> > 4. Hill and Gully
> > 5. Pack She Back to She Ma
> > 6. Tinga Layo

*Arthur Cunningham*

## ARTHUR CUNNINGHAM
### b. Nyack, New York, November 11, 1928

Cunningham, one of the more prolific current composers, began to study the piano at age six and, one year later, began to write and perform his own music. When he was twelve, he organized his own band and began writing for it. The next year, he studied composition with Wallingford Riegger and theory with Sam Morgenstern. From 1941 to 1945, he studied at the Metropolitan Music School under the guidance of Riegger and jazz musicians, Johnny Mehegan and Teddy Wilson. During this period, he often appeared on WNCY in the performance of his own works. He studied theory, timpani, and choral conducting at the summer sessions of the Juilliard School of Music in 1945 and 1946 and entered Fisk University in 1947 as a music education major where he was a pupil of John W. Work. After earning his Bachelor of Arts degree in 1951, he returned to Juilliard for two years, studying with Henry Brandt, Norman Lloyd, Peter Mennin, and Margaret Hillis.

Public performances of Cunningham's music became more frequent after 1951. During that year, under the sponsorship of the National Association of Negro Musicians, several works by Cunningham and Howard Swanson were featured. Meanwhile, he was supplying his own eighteen-piece jazz band with new works.

In 1953, he was in the Special Services of the U. S. Army, engaged in writing musical revues and television music, although he also found time to tour as the double bass player in a trio and to continue composing.

He has been closely associated with the cultural life of Rockland County, the Bear Mountain area on the west side of the Hudson River. He has played double bass with the county's Suburban Symphony Orchestra. Several works were commissioned by this orchestra.

79

Meanwhile, he took graduate work in theory and conducting at Columbia Teachers' College in New York City. In 1958 he secured his Master of Arts degree there.

Since then he has spent most of his time in composition, taking time off for lecturing at Morehouse, Spellman and Morris Brown Colleges. In addition, he served as musical director and arranger for various programs in the New York area and for the 1968 Festival of Contemporary Music, sponsored by the Rockefeller Foundation, which was held in Atlanta with Robert Shaw and the Atlanta Symphony Orchestra.

A member of ASCAP, Cunningham has written for nearly every medium. In addition to his compositions listed here, Cunningham has written approximately four hundred ballads in the jazz and rock veins and special material for singers in the media of musical show and revue and television. For the one-act opera, *House By the Sea*, (as yet unfinished), he served as librettist.

*Sources:*
> Information submitted by composer
> An
> ASCAP 1966
> Cl
> Roa
> SoA
> SoM
> Wh
> Who-A
> *Who's Who in the East*, 15th edition, 1975-1976, Chicago, Illinois, Marquis

*Unpublished works available from composer [Cunningham Music Corporation]*

**1   ADAGIO (1954)**

For oboe and string orchestra

> *Commissioned:*
>> By the Suburban Symphony of Rockland County, Suffern,
>> New York
>
> *Unpublished*
>
> *Duration:*
>> 6 minutes
>
> *First performance:*
>> 1954; Suffern, New York, Suburban Symphony of
>> Rockland County

**2   AMEN, AMEN (1965)**

For chorus (SATB), unaccompanied

> *Commission and dedication:*
>> Unitarian Church in Pomona, New York for installation of
>> new minister
>
> *Unpublished*
>
> *Duration:*
>> 3 minutes
>
> *First performance:*
>> 1965; Pomona, New York, Unitarian Church; composer, conductor
>
> *Note:*
>> Canon between chorus and bell on the church

**3   ASLEEP MY LOVE.** *See* **FOUR SONGS**

**4   BALLET (1968)**

For string quartet with jazz quartet

> *Commissioned:*
>> By French shoe manufacturers
>
> *Unpublished*
>
> *Duration:*
>> 30 minutes
>
> *First performance:*
>> February 1968; New York City; Circle in the Square; composer
>> at the piano and conducting

**5  BASIS (1968)**
For four double basses

>*Unpublished*
>*Duration:*
>>9 minutes
>
>*In five units*
>*First performance:*
>>1971; Montclair, New Jersey; members of the New Jersey
>>State Orchestra
>
>*Note:*
>>Excerpted from *Concentrics*

**6  THE BEAUTY PART (1963)**
A musical show with piano accompaniment (improvised)

>*Text:*
>>By S. J. Perelman
>
>*Unpublished*
>*Duration:*
>>1 hour 30 minutes
>
>*First performance:*
>>Summer 1963; Blauvelt, New York; Rockland County Playhouse

**7  BEGINNERS PIANO BOOK (1964)**
Twenty-eight teaching pieces

>*Unpublished*

**8  CASEY JONES; THE BRAVE ENGINEER (1968)**
For chorus (SATB) with piano

>*Text:*
>>By Arthur Cunningham adapted from words by T. Lawrence Seibert
>
>*Publication:*
>>New York: Shapiro, Bernstein, 1968
>
>*First performance:*
>>Information unavailable
>
>*Note:*
>>Co-composed with Julian Work

9 **CONCENTRICS (1968)**
For orchestra

>*Commissioned:*
>>By Benjamin Steinberg
>
>*Unpublished:*
>>Score and orchestral material available on rental from Theodore
>>Presser, New York
>
>*Duration:*
>>19 minutes
>
>*First performance:*
>>February 2, 1969; New York City; Avery Fischer Hall; Symphony
>>of the New World; Benjamin Steinberg, conductor
>
>*Notes:*
>>Nominated for a Pulitzer Prize in 1969.
>>Review in: *New York Times*, February 3, 1969, p. 30.

10 **CONCERTO FOR DOUBLE BASS (1971)**
For double bass and orchestra

>*Unpublished:*
>>Score and orchestral material available on rental from Theodore
>>Presser, New York
>
>*Duration:*
>>16 minutes
>
>*Will be performed in 1976 by Bertrand Turetsky*
>*Will be recorded in 1976*
>
>*Note:*
>>Originally titled *The Walton Statement* and dedicated to
>>Ortiz Walton

11 **THE COSSACK (1964)**
For chorus (SATB) with piano

>*Text:*
>>By Arthur Cunningham
>
>*Unpublished*
>*Duration:*
>>8 minutes

**12  CRISPUS ATTUCKS (1976)**
For concert band

> *Commissioned:*
> By Harvard University band
> *Duration:*
> 6 minutes
> *Unpublished*
> *First performance:*
> Harvard University
> *Notes:*
> In two versions.
> Short analysis in: Everett, Thomas. "Concert Band Music By Black-American Composers," in *The Black Perspective in Music*, vol. 6, no. 2, Fall 1978, pp. 143-50.

**13  DIALOGUE FOR PIANO AND ORCHESTRA (1966)**
For piano and chamber orchestra

> *Publication:*
> Bryn Mawr, Pennsylvania: Theodore Presser, 1967 (available on rental) (IU: score)
> *Duration:*
> 10 minutes

**14  DIM DU MIM (TWILIGHT) (1968-1969)**
For English horn or oboe and chamber orchestra

> *Dedication:*
> To "The donkey who walked to Bethlehem"
> *Unpublished*
> *Duration:*
> 8 minutes
> *First performance:*
> 1971; Montclair, New Jersey; New Jersey State Orchestra

**15  ECLATETTE (1969)**
For violoncello

> *Commissioned:*
> By Earl Madison for the 1970 Chaikovskii Competition in Moscow
> *Dedication:*
> To William Grant Still

*Publication:*

Nyack, New York; Cunningham Music, 1975. In *The Black Perspective in Music,* vol. 3, no. 2, May 1975, pp. 226-34

*Duration:*

12 minutes

*Notes:*

Title means "a small explosion of a scandalous nature."

Performer must have knowledge of jazz pianists and guitarists.

**16    ENGRAMS (1969)**

For piano

*Commissioned:*

By Natalie Hinderas for her 1969-1970 tour

*Publication:*

Bryn Mawr, Pennsylvania: Theodore Presser, n.d.

*First performance:*

1970; Chicago, Illinois, NAMT Convention

*Recording:*

Desto 7102/3 (1970) (IU)

**17    EVERYWHERE I GO (1961)**

For voice and piano

*Text:*

By William Shakespeare for "A Midsummer Night's Dream"

*Unpublished*

*Duration:*

2 minutes 30 seconds

*Recording:*

King Records

*Note:*

A rock piece

**18    FIFTY STARS (1963)**

For women's chorus (SA) with piano

*Text:*

By Arthur Cunningham

*Unpublished*

*Duration:*

2 minutes

**FOUR SHADOWS.** *See* **SHADOWS, FOUR**

**FOUR SONGS.** *See* **SONGS, FOUR**

19    **FRAGMENT (1968)**
For wind instruments and percussion: 3 French horns, 3 trumpets, 3 trombones, 5 temple blocks, maracas, claves, tamborine, cymbal, snare drum, 3 timpani, bass drum

>    *Unpublished*
>    *Duration:*
>        3 minutes
>    *Note:*
>        Excerpted from *Concentrics*

20    **FROM WHERE I STAND (1950; revised 1964)**
For chorus (SATB), unaccompanied

>    *Text:*
>        By Arthur Cunningham
>    *Unpublished*
>    *Duration:*
>        3 minutes

21    **FRUITFUL TREES MORE FRUITFUL ARE (1965)**
For chorus (SATB), unaccompanied

>    *Text:*
>        By George Herbert
>    *Commission and dedication:*
>        Unitarian Church in Pomona, New York for installation of
>            new minister
>    *Unpublished*
>    *Duration:*
>        5 minutes
>    *First performance:*
>        1965; Pomona, New York; Unitarian Church; composer,
>            conductor

**22 THE GARDEN OF PHOBOS (1968)**
For chorus (SATB), unaccompanied

> *Text:*
>> Life sounds
>
> *Commissioned:*
>> By Hudson Valley Chorus
>
> *Unpublished*
>
> *Duration:*
>> 12 minutes
>
> *First performance:*
>> March 2, 1969; Suffern, New York; Rockland Community College

**23 THE GINGERBREAD MAN (1955; revised 1964)**
For men's chorus (TTBB) with piano

> *Text:*
>> By Arthur Cunningham
>
> *Commissioned:*
>> By Karamu House, Cleveland, Ohio
>
> *Unpublished*
>
> *Duration:*
>> 8 minutes

**24 HAITIAN PLAY DANCES, TWO (1951)**
For 2 pianos, 4 hands

> *Unpublished*
>
> *Duration:*
>> 4 minutes
>
> *First performance:*
>> 1951; New York City; St. Mark's Church; National Association of Negro Musicians Concert; Arlene Shaw and composer, pianists

**HARLEM SUITE (1969—**
Ballet for chorus (SATB), solo voices, piano, electric bass, drums, orchestra, and dancers

> *Text:*
>> By Arthur Cunningham
>
> *Commissioned:*
>> By Dr. Robert Jones for the Laurentian Singers of St. Lawrence University, Canton, New York

*Publication:*

> Bryn Mawr, Pennsylvania: Theodore Presser, 1972– (items
> published separately) (piano-vocal scores; orchestral material on
> rental) (IU: item nos. 1, 2, 4, 5, 9; HU: item nos. 1, 2, 3, 4, 5)

*Duration:*

> "Full evening," 2 hours

*Contents:*

1. A Little Love
2. World Goin' Down
3. Sunday in de Evening
4. Lenox
5. Mundy Man
6. Lullabye for a Jazz Baby
7. Sugar Hill
8. Pataditas
9. Harlem is My Home
10. Hinkty Woman

*First performance:*

> April 24, 1971; Nashville, Tennessee; Fisk University

*Note:*

> Work is being continually augmented

**25    HE MET HER AT THE DOLPHIN (1963)**
For chorus (SATB) with piano

*Text:*

> By Arthur Cunningham

*Publication:*

> New York: Remick & Witmark, 1964 (IU; HU)

*Duration:*

> 4 minutes

*Note:*

> a. k. a. *Holiday*

**26    HINKTY WOMAN (1975).** *See* **HARLEM SUITE**
For chorus (SATB) with tenor solo

*Duration:*

> 4 minutes 30 seconds

**27**  **HIS NATURAL GRACE (1969)**
One-act mini rock opera

> *Text:*
>> By Arthur Cunningham
>
> *Unpublished*
> *Duration:*
>> 1 hour
>
> *Note:*
>> a. k. a *Louey, Louey*

**28**  **HONEY BROWN (1971)**
For men's chorus (TTBB), unaccompanied

> *Text:*
>> By Arthur Cunningham
>
> *Publication:*
>> Bryn Mawr, Pennsylvania: Theodore Presser, 1972 (IU; HU)
>
> *Duration:*
>> 4 minutes
>
> *Note:*
>> A Jubilee song

**29**  **HYMN OF OUR LORD AT THE LAST SUPPER (1962)**
For chorus (SATB), unaccompanied

> *Text:*
>> Bible, New Testament, St. John
>
> *Commissioned:*
>> By the Unitarian Church, Pomona, New York
>
> *Unpublished*
> *Duration:*
>> 10 minutes
>
> *First performance:*
>> Easter 1962; Pomona, New York; Unitarian Church

**30**  **I DO WANDER EVERYWHERE.** *See* **FOUR SONGS**

> *Commissioned:*
>> By Lee Bellaver

**31**  **IN THE YEAR SEVENTEEN (1965)**
For chorus (SATB), unaccompanied

> *Text:*
>> From literary comments on Hiroshima
>
> *Commissioned:*
>> By the Unitarian Church, Pomona, New York
>
> *Unpublished*
> *Duration:*
>> 8 minutes
>
> *First performance:*
>> Easter 1965; Pomona, New York; Unitarian Church

**32**  **INTO MY HEART (1964)**
For chorus (SATB) with piano

> *Text:*
>> By Alfred Edward Housman
>
> *Unpublished*
> *Duration:*
>> 2 minutes

**33**  **INVENTIONS, TWO (1952)**
For 2 double basses

> *Unpublished*
> *Duration:*
>> 3 minutes

**34**  **JABBERWOCKY (1960)**
For voice (soprano) and piano

> *Text:*
>> By Lewis Carroll from *Alice in Wonderland*
>
> *Commissioned:*
>> By Joy Barker
>
> *Unpublished*
> *Duration:*
>> 2 minutes 30 seconds
>
> *First performance:*
>> 1960; Spring Valley, New York; Community Music School;
>> Joy Barker, soprano

**35**  **JILL ELLEN (1975)**
For violin, viola, violoncello, and guitar

> *Unpublished*
> *Duration:*
>> 5 minutes
> *First performance:*
>> 1975; Nyack, New York; Nyack College

**36**  **JILL ELLEN (1977)**
For guitar

> *Dedication:*
>> To Jill Abrams
> *Unpublished*
> *Duration:*
>> 5 minutes
> *First performance:*
>> March 1977; Nyack, New York; Nyack College; Pardington Hall;
>> Terry Staub, guitar
> *Note:*
>> Tape available from composer

**37**  **LEAD US STILL AND GUIDE US (1965)**
Hymn for chorus (SATB) and organ

> *Text:*
>> By Arthur Cunningham
> *Commissioned:*
>> By the Unitarian Church, Pomona, New York
> *Unpublished*
> *Duration:*
>> 5 minutes
> *First performance:*
>> 1965; Pomona, New York; Unitarian Church

**38**  **THE LEADEN EYED (1956)**
For voice (soprano) and piano

> *Text:*
>> By Vachel Lindsay
> *Unpublished*

*Duration:*
>3 minutes

*First performance:*
>Early 1960's; Nyack, New York; Rockland Foundation;
>Joy Barker, soprano

**39    LENOX (1970).** *See* **HARLEM SUITE**
For chorus (SATB) with narrator and piano

>*Duration:*
>>3 minutes 30 seconds

**40    LET THE DAY BEGIN (1964)**
For women's chorus (SA), unaccompanied

>*Text:*
>>By Arthur Cunningham
>*Unpublished*
>*Duration:*
>>3 minutes

**41    LIGHTS ACROSS THE HUDSON (1956)**
For orchestra

>*Unpublished*
>*Duration:*
>>4 minutes 30 seconds
>*First performance:*
>>1957; New York City; Columbia University
>*Note:*
>>Tone poem

**42    LITANY (1972)**
For chorus (SATB) and orchestra

>*Text:*
>>By Arthur Cunningham
>*Commissioned:*
>>By Dr. Robert Jones for the summer chorus of Stanford University
>*Dedication:*
>>"to the flower children"

*Unpublished*
*Duration:*
>10 minutes
*First performance:*
>Date ?; Stanford, California; Stanford University; composer,
>conductor

**43 A LITTLE LOVE (1970).** *See* **HARLEM SUITE**
For chorus (SATB) with piano

>*Duration:*
>>4 minutes 30 seconds

**44 LORD, LOOK DOWN.** *See* **TWO PRAYERS**

**45 THE LOVELIEST OF TREES (1964)**
For chorus (SATB), unaccompanied

>*Text:*
>>By Alfred Edward Housman
>*Unpublished*
>*Duration:*
>>2 minutes

**46 LOVERS AND MADMEN.** *See* **FOUR SONGS**

**47 LULLABYE FOR A JAZZ BABY (1969).** *See* **HARLEM SUITE**
For orchestra

>*Duration:*
>>6 minutes 30 seconds
>*Recording:*
>>Desto 7107 (1970) (IU)
>*Notes:*
>>Written for Andre Kostelanetz.
>>This work has received numerous performances.
>>Review in: *The Black Perspective in Music*, vol. 4, no. 3, Fall
>>1976, p. 343.

**48** **MINAKESH (1969)**
a. For oboe and piano
b. For violoncello and strings
c. For voice and piano (1970) (vocalise)

> *Unpublished*
> *Duration:*
>> 5 minutes
> *First performance:*
>> (Voice and piano): December 15, 1970; Washington, D.C.;
>>> National Gallery of Art; Louise Parker, contralto
> *Note:*
>> Title means conjurer for good or evil

**49** **MUNDY MAN (1970).** *See* **HARLEM SUITE**
For chorus (SATB), orchestra, and harmonica

> *Duration:*
>> 3 minutes 30 seconds
> *Notes:*
>> Blues composition.
>> This work has received numerous performances

**50** **NIGHT BIRD (1978)**
For jazz quintet, solo voice, and chamber orchestra

> *Text:*
>> By Arthur Cunningham
> *Dedication:*
>> To Benjamin Breggin
> *Commissioned:*
>> By James Frazier for the A. M. E. Zion Church, Philadelphia,
>>> Pennsylvania
> *Unpublished*
> *Duration:*
>> 12 minutes
> *First performance:*
>> November 12, 1978; Carson, California; California State
>>> University; Bill Renee Jazz Ensemble; Sue Harmon, soprano;
>>> Francis Steiner, conductor

**51  NIGHT LIGHTS (1955)**

For orchestra

> *Unpublished*
> *Duration:*
>> 4 minutes

**52  NIGHT SONG (1973)**

Theater piece for chorus (SATB), soloists, and orchestra

> *Text:*
>> Swahili; Gulla from Sea Islands; and English
>
> *Commissioned:*
>> By Cheyney State College, Cheyney, Pennsylvania
>
> *Publication:*
>> New York: Theodore Presser, 1974
>
> *Duration:*
>> 1 hour 30 minutes
>
> *Contents:*
>> 1. Utumbuizo (Lullabye)
>> 2. Kai (Truth)
>> 3. Toa (Producer of Tomorrow)

**53  OCTET (1968)**

For percussion ensemble: timpani, snare drum, tambourine, suspended cymbal, triangle, guiro, maracas, claves, bass drum, 5 temple blocks, and 4 timbales

> *Dedication:*
>> To the percussion section of the Oklahoma City Symphony
>>> Orchestra
>
> *Unpublished*
> *Duration:*
>> 2 minutes
>
> *Note:*
>> Excerpted from *Concentrics*

**54  OMNUS (1968)**

For string orchestra

> *Unpublished*
> *Duration:*
>> 6 minutes
>
> *Three movements*
> *Note:*
>> Excerpted from *Concentrics*

**55 ORGAN PRELUDE (1965)**

> *Commissioned:*
>> By the Unitarian Church, Pomona, New York
>
> *Unpublished*
> *Duration:*
>> 2 minutes
>
> *First performance:*
>> 1965; Pomona, New York; Unitarian Church

**56 OSTRICH FEATHERS (1964)**
a musical play for children; for piano and improvising combo: electric bass, drums, vibraphones, and guitar

> *Text:*
>> By Barbara Brenner
>
> *Unpublished:*
>> Libretto and score available on rental from Theodore Presser, New York
>
> *Duration:*
>> 1 hour 10 minutes
>
> *First performance:*
>> October 1965; New York City; Martinique Theater
>
> *Notes:*
>> A rock musical.
>> Combo parts are not written out; they are improvised from piano part.

**57 PALE MOONS RISE IN ENDLESS CALM (1955; revised 1964)**
For chorus (SATB), unaccompanied

> *Text:*
>> By Arthur Cunningham
>
> *Unpublished*
> *Duration:*
>> 5 minutes

**58 PATADITOS (1970).** *See* **HARLEM SUITE**
For piano and orchestra

> *Duration:*
>> 5 minutes
>
> *Note:*
>> Title means "Little Kicks"

**59  PATSY PATCH AND SUSAN'S DREAM (1963)**
A rock musical for children

> *Text:*
>> By Arthur Cunningham
>
> *Unpublished*
> *Duration:*
>> 1 hour
>
> *First performance:*
>> 1963; Orangeburg, New York, an elementary school
>
> *Note:*
>> Composer also designed costumes and includes instructions for direction of play

**60  PERIMETERS (1965)**
For flute, clarinet, vibraphone, and double bass

> *Unpublished*
> *Duration:*
>> 11 minutes
>
> *Contents (four movements):*
>> 1. Arc
>> 2. Radius
>> 3. Circumference
>> 4. Diameter

**61  PIANO PIECES, SIXTY (1965)**

> *Unpublished*
> *Note:*
>> A research project on small forms for children

**PRAYERS, TWO (1970)**
For chorus (SATB) with solo voice, unaccompanied

> *Dedication:*
>> To the Fisk Jubilee Singers for their 100th anniversary
>
> *Publication:*
>> Bryn Mawr, Pennsylvania: Theodore Presser, 1972 (HU)
>
> *Contents:*
>> 1. Lord, Look Down (30 seconds)
>> 2. We Gonna Make It (30 seconds)
>
> *First performance:*
>> October 6, 1970; Nashville, Tennessee; Fisk University; Fisk Jubilee Singers

**THE PRINCE.** *See* **PROMETHEUS**

62  **PROMETHEUS (1964; revised 1965)**
For voice and piano

> *Text:*
>> By Aeschylus; translated by A. E. Havelock; adapted by
>> Arthur Cunningham
>
> *Unpublished:*
>> Score and orchestral parts available on rental from Theodore
>> Presser, New York (under title *The Prince*)
>
> *Duration:*
>> 23 minutes 30 seconds
>
> *Tape made in 1968 available from composer*
>
> *Notes:*
>> Orchestrated in 1967.
>> Later retitled *The Prince.*
>> About a Black slave prince ready to be sold and how he feels
>> about man's inhumanity.

63  **PURPLE GRAPES, GREEN FIGS, AND MULBERRIES.** *See* **FOUR SONGS**

64  **RING OUT WILD BELLS (1965)**
For chorus (SATB) and children's voices with piano

> *Text:*
>> By Alfred, Lord Tennyson
>
> *Commissioned:*
>> By a Presbyterian church in New York City
>
> *Unpublished*
>
> *Duration:*
>> 5 minutes
>
> *Note:*
>> For New Year's Eve

65  **ROOSTER RHAPSODY (1975)**
For orchestra and narrator

> *Text:*
>> By Barbara Brenner
>
> *To be published by Theodore Presser, Bryn Mawr, Pennsylvania*

*Duration:*
    17 minutes
*Version for rock quartet (12 minutes) will be recorded by RCA*
*Note:*
    Work is for children

**66  SEPTET (1968)**

For piccolo, flute, oboe, clarinet, bass clarinet, English horn, and bassoon

*Unpublished*
*Duration:*
    3 minutes
*Note:*
    Excerpted from *Concentrics*

**67  SERENADE (1950)**

For violoncello and piano

*Unpublished*
*Duration:*
    4 minutes
*First performance:*
    1950; Nashville, Tennessee; Fisk University; Bessye Atkins, cello

**68  SHADOWS, FOUR (1950)**

For piano

*Unpublished*
*Duration:*
    30 seconds
*First performance:*
    1950; Nashville, Tennessee; Fisk University; composer at the piano

**69  SHANGO (1969)**

Incidental music for a play; for African instruments

*Unpublished*
*Duration:*
    45 minutes
*Numerous performances in various school systems*

**70**  **SING CHILDREN SING (1964)**
For chorus (SATB), unaccompanied

> *Unpublished*
> *Duration:*
>> 1 minute

**SIXTY PIANO PIECES.**  *See* **PIANO PIECES, SIXTY**

**71**  **SONG OF SONGS (1951)**
For voice and piano

> *Text:*
>> By Wilfred Owen
> *Commissioned:*
>> By Joy Barker
> *Unpublished*
> *Duration:*
>> 3 minutes
> *First performance:*
>> 1951; New York City; St. Mark's Church; National Association of Negro Musicians Concert; Joy Barker, soprano

**SONGS, FOUR (1967)**
For voice (soprano) and piano

> *Texts:*
>> By William Shakespeare from "A Midsummer Night's Dream"
> *Unpublished*
> *Contents:*
>> 1. Purple Grapes, Green Figs, and Mulberries (3 minutes)
>> 2. Asleep My Love (5 minutes)
>> 3. I Do Wander Everywhere (2 minutes)
>> 4. Lovers and Madmen (2 minutes)
> *First performance:*
>> March 19, 1969; New York City; Composers Theatre, Studio 58
> *Note:*
>> Serial technique employed

**72**  **STUDIES FOR SINGING THE BLUES**
A manual for singers

> *Publication:*
>> Bryn Mawr, Pennsylvania: Theodore Presser, 1972 (NYPL)

**73**  **SUGAR HILL (1969).** *See* **HARLEM SUITE**
For piano

> *Duration:*
>> 4 minutes
> *Notes:*
>> This work is the middle section of *Lullabye for a Jazz Baby.*
>> Version for 2 double basses and violoncello (1969).

**74**  **SUN BIRD (1974-1975)**
For voice, chamber orchestra, and guitar

> *Text:*
>> By Arthur Cunningham
> *Commissioned:*
>> By Cary McMurran
> *Unpublished*
> *Duration:*
>> 17 minutes
> *First performance:*
>> March 1975; Hampton, Virginia; Hampton Roads Coliseum
> *Note:*
>> Written for Charlie Byrd and Louise Parker

**75**  **SUNDAY IN DE EVENIN' (1970).** *See* **HARLEM SUITE**
For women's chorus (SA) with piano

> *Duration:*
>> 4 minutes

**76**  **SUNDAY STONE (1973)**
For chorus (SATB) with piano or organ

> *Text:*
>> By Arthur Cunningham
> *Dedication:*
>> To Dr. David Liebler
> *Publication:*
>> Bryn Mawr, Pennsylvania: Theodore Presser, 1974
> *Duration:*
>> 4 minutes
> *First performance:*
>> Easter 1973; Canton, New York; St. Lawrence University;
>>> Robert Jones, conductor
> *Note:*
>> Review of work in: *The Black Perspective in Music,* Fall 1975, p. 341

**77    THEATRE PIECE (1966)**
For orchestra

> *Unpublished*
> *Duration:*
>> 10 minutes
> *First performance:*
>> 1968; Atlanta, Georgia; Spellman College; Festival of Contemporary Music; Atlanta Symphony Orchestra

**78    THEN THE CRICKET SINGS (1957; revised 1964)**
For chorus (SATB) and solo voice with piano

> *Text:*
>> By Arthur Cunningham
> *Unpublished*
> *Duration:*
>> 1 minute
> *First performance:*
>> October 1957; New York City; Columbia Teachers College

**79    THIS LOVE IS TRUE LOVE (1961)**
For voice and piano

> *Text:*
>> By Arthur Cunningham
> *Unpublished*
> *Duration:*
>> 2 minutes 30 seconds
> *Recording:*
>> King Records

**80    THISBY DYING (1968)**
For flute and violoncello or violoncello alone

> *Unpublished*
> *Duration:*
>> 5 minutes
> *First performance:*
>> Date ?; Norfolk, Virginia; Virginia State College; Antoinette Handy, flute

*Recording:*
> Eastern ERS-513 (1972)

*Notes:*
> This work is an arrangement of *Asleep My Love* from *Four Songs*.
> Later arranged for flute and viola (1975) and performed in
> Spring 1976.


**81  TIMBER (1971)**
For chorus (SATB), unaccompanied

> *Text:*
>> By Arthur Cunningham
>
> *Publication:*
>> Bryn Mawr, Pennsylvania: Theodore Presser, 1972 (IU; HU)
>
> *Duration:*
>> 2 minutes
>
> *Note:*
>> A Jubilee song


**82  TRINITIES (1969)**
For violoncello and 2 double basses

> *Commissioned:*
>> By Arthur Davis
>
> *Unpublished*
> *Duration:*
>> 15 minutes
>
> *Contents:*
>> 1. Statement
>> 2. Hymn
>> 3. Strut (Jubilee)


**83  TRIO FOR FLUTE, VIOLA, AND BASSOON (1952)**

> *Unpublished*
> *Duration:*
>> 3 minutes
>
> *First performance:*
>> 1952; New York City; Juilliard School of Music; student ensemble

**84   TRIO FOR VIOLIN, VIOLA, AND VIOLONCELLO (1968)**

> *Unpublished*
> *Duration:*
> > 10 minutes
> *Three movements*
> *Note:*
> > Excerpted from *Concentrics*

**85   TURNING OF THE BABIES IN THE BED (1951)**
For voice (baritone) and piano

> *Text:*
> > By Paul Laurence Dunbar
> *Unpublished*
> *Duration:*
> > 5 minutes
> *First performance:*
> > 1951; New York City; St. Mark's Church; National Association of Negro Musicians Concert

**TWO HAITIAN PLAY DANCES.** *See* **HAITIAN PLAY DANCES, TWO**

**TWO INVENTIONS.** *See* **INVENTIONS, TWO**

**TWO PRAYERS.** *See* **PRAYERS, TWO**

**86   TWO WORLD SUITE (1971)**
For 6 double basses

> *Unpublished*
> *Duration:*
> > 4 minutes
> *Note:*
> > a. k. a. *Strut*

**VIOLETS AND PHOSPHER.** *See* **VIOLETTA**

**87   VIOLETTA (1963)**
A musical for soprano, tenor, baritone, and bass with string quartet and string octet

> *Text:*
> > By Odiberti; adaptation of his play "Le Mal Coeur"

*Unpublished:*
>LC: piano-vocal score

*Duration:*
>2 hours

*Note:*
>a. k. a. *Violets and Phospher*


**THE WALTON STATEMENT.** *See* **CONCERTO FOR DOUBLE BASS**


88  **WE GONNA MAKE IT.** *See* **TWO PRAYERS**


89  **THE WEST WIND (1962)**
For chorus (SATB), unaccompanied .

*Text:*
>By John Masefield

*Unpublished*
*Duration:*
>10 minutes


90  **WHEN I WAS ONE AND TWENTY (1963)**
For chorus (SATB) with piano

*Text:*
>By Alfred Edward Housman

*Unpublished*
*Duration:*
>3 minutes


91  **WITH RUE MY HEART IS LADEN (1964)**
For chorus (SATB), unaccompanied

*Text:*
>By Alfred Edward Housman

*Unpublished*
*Duration:*
>1 minute


92  **WORLD GOIN' DOWN (1972).** *See* **HARLEM SUITE**
For chorus (SATB) with soprano and alto solos

*William L. Dawson, composer-conductor*

## WILLIAM LEVI DAWSON
*b. Anniston, Alabama, September 26, 1899*


Professor Dawson, one of the most accomplished and successful of Black composers and educators, entered the Tuskegee Institute in 1914, where he soon attracted the interest of Booker T. Washington who was then president of the Institute. Various tasks, including music library work, provided him with an income while at Tuskegee. During this time he was a student of Frank L. Drye in instrumental performance and Alice Carter Simmons in harmony. He left the Institute after his graduation in 1921 to spend a year at Washburn College in Topeka, Kansas, where he studied composition with Henry V. Stearns. From 1922 to 1925, he attended the Horner Institute of Fine Arts in Kansas City, continuing his composition studies with Carl Busch and Regina G. Hall. After securing his Bachelor of Music degree in 1925, he moved to Chicago and enrolled at the American Conservatory of Music for composition study with Adolph Weidig. He earned his Master of Music degree in 1927 and remained in Chicago to study with Thorvald Otterstrom and later with Felix Borowski at the Chicago Musical College. Additional graduate work was taken at the Eastman School of Music in Rochester, New York.

During his student years he was active as an instrumentalist, appearing as first trombonist under Frederick Stock in the Chicago Civic Orchestra from 1926 to 1930, and touring the Redpath Chautauqua Circuit in New England in 1921. He served as director of music at Topeka's Kansas Vocational College from 1921 to 1922 and at the Lincoln High School in Kansas City from 1922 to 1925.

From 1931 until his resignation in 1955, Dawson was head of the School of Music at Tuskegee Institute, establishing the school's curricular program in music.

The Tuskegee Choir which he began directing in 1932 toured throughout the United States for many years and gave such memorable performances as the opening of Radio City Music Hall, December 27, 1932, a 1933 appearance at the White House at the invitation of President Herbert Hoover, and participation in the birthday festivities for President-elect Franklin D. Roosevelt in the same year. In addition, the choir performed on numerous radio and television broadcasts over all three major networks. Frequently included on its programs were the larger works of Samuel Coleridge-Taylor. Several recordings were made by the Tuskegee Choir of Dawson's arrangements of spirituals.

In 1930 and 1931, Dawson won the Rodman Wanamaker Contests for composition for his *Scherzo* for orchestra and *Lovers Plighted.* One of the first major performances of Dawson's music took place in 1934 when the Philadelphia Orchestra under Leopold Stokowski premiered the *Negro Folk Symphony,* a work which has had numerous subsequent performances by Stokowski as well as other conductors.

In 1952-1953 he took a sabbatical leave and went to Western Africa to study the native music of several countries there. Upon his return he resumed his activity with the Tuskegee Choir, appearing frequently on television and in concert. After his retirement in 1955 he was awarded an honorary doctorate in music by the Tuskegee Institute shortly before the U. S. Department of State sent him to Spain as a choral conductor. To a large extent, his activities since his resignation have centered on guest conductor appearances, lectures, and consultations. He was inducted into the Alabama Hall of Fame in 1975.

*Sources:*

Information submitted by composer

An

Ba

Braithwaite, Coleridge Alexander. *A Survey of the Lives and Creative Activities of Some Negro Composers,* dissertation, New York, Teachers' College, Columbia University, 1952

Cl

Ewen, David. *American Composers Today,* New York: H. W. Wilson, 1949

Har

Harris, Carl G, Jr. "Three Schools of Black Choral Composers and Arrangers," in *Choral Journal,* April 1974, pp. 11-18

Howard, John Tasker. *Our Contemporary Composers,* New York: Crowell, 1941

I-Who 1944, 1949, 1964, 10th edition, 1975

NYB 1952

Reis, Claire R. *Composers in America,* New York: Macmillan, 1947

Rob

Scholes, Percy A. *The Oxford Companion to Music,* London: Oxford University Press, 1947, 10th edition, 1970

SoA

SoM

Th

To

Weir, Albert E. *The Macmillan Encyclopedia of Music and Musicians,* New York: Macmillan, 1938

Wh

Who-A

*Who's Who in America*, 40th edition, 1978-1979, Chicago, Illinois, Marquis

*Who's Who in the South and Southwest,* 1973-1974, Chicago, Illinois, Marquis

**1a AIN'A THAT GOOD NEWS (1934)**
For chorus (SATB), unaccompanied

> *Text:*
>> Spiritual
> *Publication:*
>> Music Press of Tuskegee Institute, 1937 (HU; IU; LC)
> *Duration:*
>> 1 minute
> *Recordings:*
>> Black Heritage, vol. 2 (1970)
>> Westminster W-9633 (1968) (IU)
>> Tape in IU Library (IU performance)

**1b AIN'A THAT GOOD NEWS**
For men's chorus (TTBB), unaccompanied

> *Publication:*
>> Music Press of Tuskegee Institute, 1937 (HU; LC)

**1c AIN'A THAT GOOD NEWS**
For women's chorus (SSAA), unaccompanied

> *Publication:*
>> Music Press of Tuskegee Institute

**2 BEFORE THE SUN GOES DOWN**
For chorus (SATB) and piano

> *Publication:*
>> Park Ridge, Illinois: Kjos Music Co., 1978
> *Note:*
>> To the tune *Londonderry Air*

**3 BEHOLD THE STAR (1946)**
For chorus (SATB), echo chorus, soprano and tenor solos, unaccompanied

> *Text:*
>> Spiritual
> *Publication:*
>> Music Press of Tuskegee Institute, 1946 (HU)
> *Duration:*
>> 4 minutes 30 seconds
> *Recordings:*
>> Black Heritage, vol. 2 (1970) (IU)
>> Westminster W-9633 (1968) (IU)

**4   BREAK, BREAK, BREAK (1930)**
For chorus and orchestra


**5a   EVERY TIME I FEEL THE SPIRIT (1946)**
For chorus (SATB) with baritone solo, unaccompanied

> *Text:*
>> Spiritual
> *Publication:*
>> Music Press of Tuskegee Institute, 1946 (HU; LC)
> *Duration:*
>> 1 minute 40 seconds
> *Recordings:*
>> Black Heritage, vol. 2 (1970) (IU)
>> Westminster W-9633 (1968) (IU)


**5b   EVERY TIME I FEEL THE SPIRIT**
For men's chorus (TTBB), unaccompanied

> *Publication:*
>> Music Press of Tuskegee Institute, 1966 (HU; LC)


**5c   EVERY TIME I FEEL THE SPIRIT (1946; revised 1966)**
For women's chorus (SSAA), unaccompanied

> *Publication:*
>> Music Press of Tuskegee Institute, 1966 (HU; LC)


**6   EZEKIEL SAW DE WHEEL (1942)**
For chorus (SATB), unaccompanied

> *Text:*
>> Spiritual
> *Publication:*
>> Music Press of Tuskegee Institute, 1942 (HU; IU; LC)
> *Duration:*
>> 2 minutes 16 seconds
> *Recordings:*
>> Black Heritage, vol. 2 (1970) (IU)
>> Westminster W-9633 (1968) (IU)

**7a  FEED-A MY SHEEP**
For chorus (SATB) and piano

> *Text:*
>> By G. Lake Imes
>
> *Publication:*
>> Music Press of Tuskegee Institute, 1971 (HU; IU; LC)

**7b  FEED-A MY SHEEP**
For men's chorus (TTBB) and piano

> *Publication:*
>> Music Press of Tuskegee Institute, 1971 (HU; IU)

**7c  FEED-A MY SHEEP**
For women's chorus (SSAA) and piano

> *Publication:*
>> Music Press of Tuskegee Institute, 1971 (HU; IU)

**8  FOREVER THINE**
For voice (medium) and piano

> *Text:*
>> By William Levi Dawson
>
> *Published:*
>> By composer at Tuskegee Institute, 1920 (HU)

**9a  GO TO SLEEP**
For chorus (SATB), unaccompanied

> *Text:*
>> By Vernon N. Ray
>
> *Publication:*
>> Chicago: FitzSimons, 1926 (HU) (out of print)

**9b  GO TO SLEEP**
For women's chorus (SSA), unaccompanied

> *Publication:*
>> Chicago: FitzSimons, 1926 (out of print)

**10a** **HAIL MARY (1946)**
For chorus (SATB), unaccompanied

> *Text:*
> > Spiritual
> *Publication:*
> > Music Press of Tuskegee Institute, 1946 (HU)
> *Duration:*
> > 3 minutes 28 seconds
> *Recordings:*
> > Black Heritage, vol. 2 (1970) (IU)
> > Westminster W-9633 (1968) (IU)

**10b** **HAIL MARY**
For men's chorus, unaccompanied

> *Publication:*
> > Music Press of Tuskegee Institute, 1946 (HU)

**11** **I COULDN'T HEAR NOBODY PRAY**
For chorus (SATB) with soprano solo, unaccompanied

> *Text:*
> > Spiritual
> *Publication:*
> > Chicago: FitzSimons, 1926 (HU)
> *Duration:*
> > 2 minutes 43 seconds
> *Recording:*
> > Westminster W-9633 (1968) (IU)

**12a** **I WAN' TO BE READY**
For chorus (SATB) with alto and baritone solos, unaccompanied

> *Text:*
> > Spiritual
> *Publication:*
> > Music Press of Tuskegee Institute, 1967 (HU; IU)
> *Duration:*
> > 1 minute 48 seconds
> *Recording:*
> > Westminster W-9633 (1968) (IU)

**12b I WAN' TO BE READY**
For men's chorus (TTBB) with tenor and baritone solos, unaccompanied

> *Publication:*
> Music Press of Tuskegee Institute, 1967 (HU; IU)

**12c I WAN' TO BE READY**
For women's chorus (SSAA) with soprano and alto solos, unaccompanied

> *Publication:*
> Music Press of Tuskegee Institute, 1967 (HU; IU)

**13a IN HIS CARE-O**
For chorus (SATB), unaccompanied

> *Text:*
> Spiritual
> *Publication:*
> Music Press of Tuskegee Institute, 1961 (HU; IU; LC)

**13b IN HIS CARE-O**
For men's chorus (TTBB), unaccompanied

> *Publication:*
> Music Press of Tuskegee Institute, 1961 (HU; LC)

**14 INTERLUDE**
For piano

> *Manuscript* (NYPL)

**15a JESUS WALKED THIS LONESOME VALLEY**
For voice and piano

> *Text:*
> Spiritual
> *Publication:*
> Chicago: Gamble Hinged Music, 1927 (HU) (distributed by
> Warner Bros. Music, New York)
> *Duration:*
> 3 minutes 20 seconds
> *Recordings:*
> Black Heritage, vol. 2 (1970) (IU)
> Narthex 827N-4581

**15b  JESUS WALKED THIS LONESOME VALLEY**
For chorus (SATB) and piano

> *Publication:*
>> New York: Remick, 1927 (HU) (distributed by Warner Bros.
>> Music, New York)

**15c  JESUS WALKED THIS LONESOME VALLEY**
For women's chorus (SSAA) and (SSA) and piano

> *Publication:*
>> New York: Remick, 1927 (LC) (distributed by Warner Bros.
>> Music, New York)

**15d  JESUS WALKED THIS LONESOME VALLEY**
For men's chorus (TTBB) and piano

> *Publication:*
>> New York: Remick, 1927 (distributed by Warner Bros. Music,
>> New York)

**16  JUMP BACK, HONEY, JUMP BACK**
For voice and piano

> *Text:*
>> By Paul Laurence Dunbar
> *Publication:*
>> Kansas City, Missouri: Wunderlichs Piano, 1923 (LC)
> *Note:*
>> Won Wanamaker Prize in 1930

**17a  KING JESUS IS A-LISTENING**
For chorus (SATB), unaccompanied

> *Text:*
>> Negro folk song
> *Publication:*
>> Chicago: FitzSimons, 1925 (HU)
> *Duration:*
>> 2 minutes
> *Recordings:*
>> Black Heritage, vol. 2 (1970) (IU)
>> Westminster W-9366 (1968) (IU)

**17b  KING JESUS IS A-LISTENING**
For men's chorus (TTBB), unaccompanied

> *Publication:*
> Chicago: FitzSimons, 1929

**17c  KING JESUS IS A-LISTENING**
For women's chorus (SSA), unaccompanied

> *Publication:*
> Chicago: FitzSimons, 1946

**18  LIT'L BOY-CHILE**
For chorus (SATB) with soprano and alto (or baritone) solos, unaccompanied

> *Text:*
> Spiritual
> *Publication:*
> Music Press of Tuskegee Institute, 1942 (HU; IU; LC)
> *Duration:*
> 3 minutes 11 seconds
> *Recording:*
> Black Heritage, vol. 2 (1970) (IU)

**19  LOVERS PLIGHTED**
For chorus (SATB)

> *Note:*
> Won Wanamaker Prize in 1931

**20a  MARY HAD A BABY**
For chorus (SATB) with soprano solo, unaccompanied

> *Text:*
> Spiritual
> *Dedication:*
> To Robert Shaw
> *Publication:*
> Music Press of Tuskegee Institute, 1947 (HU; LC)
> *Duration:*
> 1 minute 55 seconds
> *Recordings:*
> Black Heritage, vol. 2 (1970) (IU)
> Westminster W-9633 (1968) (IU)
> Carillon Records LP-101

**20b** **MARY HAD A BABY**
For men's chorus (TTBB) with tenor solo, unaccompanied

> *Publication:*
> Music Press of Tuskegee Institute, 1947 (HU; LC)

**THE MONGREL YANK.** *See* **THE RUGGED YANK**

**21a** **MY LORD WHAT A MOURNING**
For voice (low) and piano

> *Text:*
> Spiritual (Bible, New Testament, Matthew 24:29)
> *Dedication:*
> To Marian Anderson
> *Publication:*
> Chicago: FitzSimons, 1927 (HU; LC)

**21b** **MY LORD WHAT A MOURNING**
For chorus (SATB), unaccompanied

> *Publication:*
> Chicago: FitzSimons, 1926 (HU)

**22** **NEGRO FOLK SYMPHONY (1931; revised 1952)**
For orchestra

> *Publication:*
> Delaware Water Gap, Pennsylvania: Shawnee Music, 1965
> (Miniature score: IU; LC; NYPL)
> *Duration:*
> 35 minutes
> *Three Movements:*
> The Bond of Africa
> Hope in the Night
> O Le' Me Shine, Shine Like a Morning Star
> *First performance:*
> November 14, 1934, Philadelphia, Pennsylvania: Philadelphia
> Orchestra; Leopold Stokowski, conductor

*Recording:*

Decca DL 710077 (revised version) (1963) (IU)

*Notes:*

Manuscript in Howard University, Moreland Collection

Reviews in: Philadelphia newspaper, November 24, 1934

*Music Journal*, October 1964, vol. 22, pp. 64-65

*Kansas City Star*, January 30, 1966

*Nashville Tennessean*, May 2, 1966

**23    A NEGRO WORK SONG FOR ORCHESTRA (1941)**

*Commissioned:*

By Columbia Broadcasting System, 1940, for American School
of the Air

*Published:*

In New York, 194- (NYPL)

*Note:*

Based on the folksong, *Stewball*

**24    OH, WHAT A BEAUTIFUL CITY**

For chorus (SATB), unaccompanied

*Text:*

Spiritual

*Publication:*

Music Press of Tuskegee Institute, 1934 (HU; LC)

*Duration:*

3 minutes 15 seconds

*Recording:*

Black Heritage, vol. 2 (1970) (IU)

**25a    OUT IN THE FIELDS**

For voice and piano (orchestra)

*Text:*

By Louise Imogen Guiney

*Publication:*

Chicago: Gamble Hinged Music, 1929 (HU) (Kjos Music Co.,
distributor)

*Duration:*

2 minutes 35 seconds

*Recording:*

Desto DC-7107 (1972) (IU) (orchestral version)

**25**  **OUT IN THE FIELDS**
b. For chorus (SATB) and piano (orchestra)
c. For women's chorus (SSA) and piano (orchestra)

>> *Dedication:*
>>> "In memory of my beloved wife, Cornella"
>> *Publication:*
>>> Music Press of Tuskegee Institute, 1957 (HU; IU) (orchestral accompaniment available on rental from Kjos Music Co.)

**26a**  **THE RUGGED YANK**
For men's chorus (TTBB) and piano

>> *Text:*
>>> By Allen Quade
>> *Publications:*
>>> Chicago: Gamble Hinged Music, 1930 (HU: under title *The Mongrel Yank*).
>>> Music Press of Tuskegee Institute, 1970 (IU).

**26b**  **THE RUGGED YANK**
For male voice and piano

>> *Publication:*
>>> Music Press of Tuskegee Institute

**27**  **SCHERZO (1930)**
For orchestra

>> *Note:*
>>> Won Wanamaker Prize in 1930

**28**  **SLUMBER SONG**
a. For chorus (SATB) and piano
b. For women's chorus (SSA) and piano
c. For women's chorus (SA) and piano
d. For men's chorus (TB) and piano

>> *Publication:*
>>> Music Press of Tuskegee Institute

**29**  **SONATA FOR VIOLIN AND PIANO (1927)**
In A major

**30a** **SOON AH WILL BE DONE (1934; revised 1962)**
For chorus (SATB), unaccompanied

> *Text:*
>> Spiritual
>
> *Publication:*
>> Music Press of Tuskegee Institute, 1934 (HU; ILL; IU; LC)
>
> *Duration:*
>> 2 minutes 45 seconds
>
> *Recording:*
>> Black Heritage, vol. 2 (1970) (IU)

**30b** **SOON AH WILL BE DONE**
For men's chorus (TTBB), unaccompanied

> *Publication:*
>> Music Press of Tuskegee Institute, 1934 (HU; ILL; LC); 1947 (IU)
>
> *Recordings:*
>> Capitol P-8431
>> Columbia AL-45
>> Monitor MP-576
>> Victor V-10-1277

**31a** **STEAL AWAY**
For chorus (SATB), unaccompanied

> *Text:*
>> Spiritual
>
> *Publication:*
>> Music Press of Tuskegee Institute, 1942 (HU; LC)

**31b** **STEAL AWAY**
For men's chorus (TTBB), unaccompanied

> *Publication:*
>> Music Press of Tuskegee Institute, 1942 (HU; ILL; LC)

**32a** **SWING LOW, SWEET CHARIOT**
For chorus (SATB) with soprano solo, unaccompanied

> *Text:*
>> Spiritual
>
> *Publication:*
>> Music Press of Tuskegee Institute, 1946 (HU; LC)

**32b  SWING LOW, SWEET CHARIOT**
For men's chorus (TTBB) with tenor solo, unaccompanied

> *Publication:*
>> Music Press of Tuskegee Institute, 1946 (HU; LC)


**32c  SWING LOW, SWEET CHARIOT**
For women's chorus (SSA) with alto solo, unaccompanied

> *Publication:*
>> Music Press of Tuskegee Institute, 1946 (HU; LC)


**33a  TALK ABOUT A CHILD THAT DO LOVE JESUS**
For voice (low) and piano

> *Text:*
>> Spiritual
> *Dedication:*
>> To Roland Hayes
> *Publication:*
>> Chicago: FitzSimons, 1927 (HU; LC)
> *Recording:*
>> Period SPL-580


**33b  TALK ABOUT A CHILD THAT DO LOVE JESUS**
For chorus (SATTBB) with soprano solo and piano

> *Publication:*
>> Chicago: FitzSimons, 1927 (HU)
> *Duration:*
>> 1 minute 41 seconds
> *Recording:*
>> Black Heritage, vol. 2 (1970) (IU)


**34a  THERE IS A BALM IN GILEAD**
For chorus (SATB), unaccompanied

> *Text:*
>> Spiritual (Bible, Old Testament Jeremiah 8:22)
> *Publication:*
>> Music Press of Tuskegee Institute, 1939 (HU; IU; LC)

*121*

*Duration:*

3 minutes 12 seconds

*Recordings:*

Black Heritage, vol. 2 (1970) (IU)

Westminster W-9633 (1968) (IU)

Tape in IU Library (IU performance)

**34b   THERE IS A BALM IN GILEAD**

For men's chorus (TTBB), unaccompanied

*Publication:*

Music Press of Tuskegee Institute, 1939 (HU; ILL; LC)

**34c   THERE IS A BALM IN GILEAD**

For women's chorus (SSAA), unaccompanied

*Publication:*

Music Press of Tuskegee Institute, 1939 (HU; LC)

**34d   THERE IS A BALM IN GILEAD**

For voice and piano

*Publication:*

Music Press of Tuskegee Institute

**35   THERE'S A LIT'L WHEEL A-TURNIN' IN MY HEART**

For chorus (SSATB), unaccompanied

*Text:*

Spiritual

*Publication:*

Music Press of Tuskegee Institute, 1949 (HU; LC)

**36   TRIO FOR VIOLIN, VIOLONCELLO AND PIANO (1925)**

In A major

**37a   YOU GOT TO REAP JUST WHAT YOU SOW**

For voice and piano

*Text:*

Spiritual

*Dedication:*
>To Paul Robeson

*Publication:*
>Chicago: Gamble Hinged Music, 1928 (HU) (distributed by
>Warner Bros. Music, New York)


**37    YOU GOT TO REAP JUST WHAT YOU SOW**
b.  For mixed chorus (SATB) and piano
c.  For women's chorus (SSAA) and piano
d.  For men's chorus (TTBB) and piano

>*Publication:*
>>New York: Remick, 1927 (distributed by Warner Bros. Music,
>>New York)


**38    ZION'S WALLS**
For chorus (SATB) with soprano solo, unaccompanied

>*Text:*
>>Spiritual

>*Publication:*
>>Music Press of Tuskegee Institute, 1961 (HU; LC)


### ARRANGEMENT

**PILGRIM'S CHORUS FROM "TANNHAUSER"**
Opera by Richard Wagner
For chorus (SATB), unaccompanied

>*Publication:*
>>Park Ridge, Illinois: Kjos Music Co.

*Roger Dickerson bowing at World Premiere of*
Orpheus an' His Slide Trombone.
*Narrator Roscoe Lee Browne on the left, and
conductor Werner Torkanowsky, the right.
March 18, 1975, New Orleans, La.*

## ROGER DICKERSON
*b. New Orleans, Louisiana, August 24, 1934*


Dickerson's career as a composer began in high school, following several years of piano study. His musical milieu at this time centered around jazz, and his first knowledge of counterpoint, harmony, and orchestration came from a relative who had played trumpet with Lionel Hampton. He graduated from Dillard University in 1955 with a Bachelor of Music degree, *cum laude*. His graduate studies were taken at Indiana University where he worked under the guidance of Bernhard Heiden, receiving his Master of Music degree in 1957. During this time, he secured public performances of several works.

After graduation, he was drafted into the armed forces and stationed for several months at Fort Chaffee in Arkansas during which time he played double bass with the Fort Smith Symphony Orchestra and worked as composer and arranger for the army band. The next several years were spent in Europe, first in Heidelberg, Germany, where, for the USAREUR Headquarters Band, he returned to jazz composition. In 1959 his tour of duty with the army ended, and he received a Fulbright Fellowship which took him to Vienna, where he studied composition with Karl Schiske and Alfred Uhl at the Akademe für Musik und Darstellende Kunst. The Fulbright award was renewed for a second year in 1960. He remained in Vienna yet another year, writing several works which secured extensive and important performances in Europe. Feeling that future compositions should reflect his cultural heritage, he returned to the United States in 1962 after his third year in Vienna. A John Hay Whitney Fellowship granted to him in 1964 allowed him to further his compositional activity. In 1965 he was elected to ASCAP, and in 1972 Dickerson composed a series of concert pieces for young string players on a commission from the Rockefeller Foundation.

A resident of New Orleans, Louisiana, Dickerson continues to compose and have his works performed. A consultant in music to the Humanities Section of the Institute for Services to Education in Washington, D. C., Dickerson has worked as a guest artist with students at many Black universities. In addition, he served as music editor for three books brought out by the Institute. In February 1978 PBS aired an hour-long documentary about his life and works.

*Sources:*
> Information submitted by composer
> An
> ASCAP 1966
> "New Orleans Concerto," in *Change,* vol. 10, no. 6,
> > June-July 1978
> "Sounding Out the Spirit of New Orleans," in *States-Item*
> > (New Orleans), April 9, 1975, Section B (Lifestyle), p. 1

**1  CHORALE PRELUDE (DAS NEUGEBORNE KINDELEIN) (1956)**

For organ

> *Unpublished* (IU)
> *Duration:*
>> 3 minutes
>
> *First performance:*
>> 1971; New Orleans, Louisiana; Dillard University; Herndon
>> Spillman, organ

**2  CONCERT OVERTURE FOR ORCHESTRA (1957)**

> *Unpublished:*
>> On rental from Southern Music Publishing Co., New York (IU)
>
> *Duration:*
>> 15 minutes
>
> *First performance:*
>> 1965; New Orleans, Louisiana; Tulane University; New Orleans
>> Philharmonic, Werner Torkanowsky, conductor
>
> *Recorded:*
>> For Voice of America in South America
>
> *Notes:*
>> Written for Masters' thesis
>> Review in: *Saturday Review,* April 17, 1965, p. 30

**3  CONCERT PIECES FOR BEGINNING STRING PLAYERS, TEN (1973)**

> *Commissioned:*
>> By the Youth String Program of the New Orleans Philharmonic
>> through a Rockefeller Foundation Grant
>
> *Publication:*
>> Southern Music Publishing Co., New York, 1977
>
> *Duration:*
>> 19 minutes
>
> *Contents:*
>> 1. Cathedral Bells
>> 2. Jubilee
>> 3. Angelic Chorus
>> 4. Dance
>> 5. Mysteries
>> 6. Song

    7. Parade of the Dragons

    8. An American Village

    9. Figures in Space

   10. The Machine Age

*First performance:*

    (Pieces 1, 5, 7, 9): 1973; New Orleans, Louisiana; Ursuline
        Academy; Youth String Orchestra; Carter Nice, conductor

*Note:*

    "The pieces provide a first ensemble experience, an opportunity
    for beginning and intermediate players to perform with more
    advanced players. The pieces are written primarily for open
    strings and first and second fingers in the first position."

**4   ESSAY FOR BAND (1958)**

For symphonic wind ensemble

*Dedication:*

    To Sergeant Brown

*To be published by Southern Music Publishing Co., New York*

*Duration:*

    10 minutes

*First performance:*

    1958; Fort Chaffee, Arkansas; 449th Army Band; composer,
    conductor

**5   FAIR DILLARD (1955)**

For chorus (SATB), unaccompanied

*Text:*

    By Joyce Nicholas

*Unpublished*

*Duration:*

    2 minutes 30 seconds

*First performance:*

    1955; New Orleans, Louisiana; Dillard University; Dillard
    University Senior Concert Choir; composer, conductor

**6   FUGUE 'N BLUES (1959)**

For big band: 4 trumpets, 5 trombones, 5 saxophones, rhythm section, solo
flute (played by 1 saxophone player)

*Unpublished*

*Duration:*
    ca. 6 min. (dependent upon length of improvisatory solos)
*First performance:*
    1959; Heidelberg, Germany; 33rd Army Band

## 7    MOVEMENT FOR TRUMPET AND PIANO (1960)

*Dedication:*
    To Gloria Shipwash
*To be published by Southern Music Publishing Co., New York*
*Duration:*
    5 minutes
*First performance:*
    1960; Vienna, Austria; Gloria Shipwash, trumpet; Robert
    Hopkins, piano

## 8    MUSIC FOR STRING TRIO (1957)

*Unpublished*
*Duration:*
    3 minutes 30 seconds

## 9    MUSIC I HEARD (1956)

For voice (soprano) and piano

*Text:*
    By Conrad Aiken
*Unpublished*
*Duration:*
    4 minutes
*First performance:*
    1956; Bloomington, Indiana; Indiana University; Carolyn Rees,
    soprano; Harvey Van Buren, piano

## 10    A MUSICAL SERVICE FOR LOUIS (A REQUIEM FOR LOUIS ARMSTRONG) (1972)

For orchestra with optional mixed chorus (no text)

*Commissioned:*
    By the New Orleans Philharmonic through a National Endowment
    for the Arts Grant
*Dedication:*
    To Louis Armstrong

*Publication:*
New York, Southern Music Publishing Co., 1973 (score) (IU; LC)
*Duration:*
15 minutes
*First performance:*
March 7, 1972; New Orleans, Louisiana; New Orleans Philharmonic;
Werner Torkanowsky, conductor
*Notes:*
Brief description in: *Second Line*, vol. 24 (Spring 1972), p. 10
Reviews in: *States-Item* (New Orleans), March 8, 1972
*Times-Picayune* (New Orleans), March 9, 1972
*Mobile Register* (Alabama), March 9, 1972
*Clarion Herald* (New Orleans), March 16, 1972
*New York Times*, February 6, 1973
*The Greensboro Record* (North Carolina), July 14, 1975
*The Greensboro Daily News*, July 14, 1975


**11   THE NEGRO SPEAKS OF RIVERS (1961)**
For voice (soprano) and piano

*Text:*
By Langston Hughes
*Unpublished*
*Duration:*
5 minutes
*First performance:*
1969; broadcast of NET's "Black Journal"; Estelle Behan, soprano;
composer at the piano
*Note:*
Vocal line can be played by flute or oboe


**12   NEW ORLEANS CONCERTO (1976)**
For piano and orchestra with soprano solo

*Commissioned:*
By Werner Torkanowsky and Alexis Weissenberg for the
bicentennial
*To be published by Southern Music Publishing Co., New York*
*Duration:*
25 minutes
*Three movements*

*First performance:*

January 14, 1977; New Orleans, Louisiana; New Orleans
Philharmonic; Werner Torkanowsky, conductor; Leon Bates,
piano

*Notes:*

Reviews in: *The Clarion Herald* (New Orleans), January, 1977
*Times-Picayune* (New Orleans), January 20, 1977
*Washington Post,* February 28, 1978

Institute for Services to Education Inc., Washington, D. C. has
released a film about the creation of this work. Presented twice
on national networks.

## 13    ORPHEUS AN' HIS SLIDE TROMBONE (1974-1975)

For orchestra and narrator

*Text:*

Based on Jeanne Greenberg's "Orpheus an' Eurydice" in *Rites of
Passage*

*Dedication:*

To Werner Torkanowsky

*To be published by Southern Music Publishing Co., New York*

*Duration:*

22 minutes

*First performance:*

March 18, 1975; New Orleans, Louisiana; New Orleans
Philharmonic; Werner Torkanowsky, conductor; Roscoe Lee
Brown, narrator

*Notes:*

Text and brief description in *New Orleans Philharmonic Symphony
Orchestra Program Notes*, March 18-19, 1975

Reviews in: *Clarion Herald* (New Orleans), April 3, 1975
*St. Paul Pioneer Press* (Minnesota), February 21, 1977

## 14    "PREKUSSION" (1954)

For percussion ensemble: triangle, wood blocks, large cymbal, tambourine, bass
drum, tom tom, side drum, castenets, timpani, and piano

*Unpublished*

*Duration:*

2 minutes

*First performance:*

1954; New Orleans, Louisiana; Dillard University; Dillard University
Percussion Ensemble

**15** **PSALM 49 (1979)**
For chorus (SATB) and 3 timpani

*Commissioned:*
By chorus of Loyola University of New Orleans, Louisiana
*Dedication:*
To Howard Swanson
*To be published by Southern Music Publishing Co., New York*
*Duration:*
11 minutes
*First performance:*
March 17, 1979; New Orleans, Louisiana; Loyola University Choir


**16** **QUINTET FOR WIND INSTRUMENTS (1961)**
For woodwind quintet

*To be published by Southern Music Publishing Co., New York*
*Duration:*
10 minutes
*In one movement*
*First performance:*
1961; Vienna, Austria; Musik Akademie Bläserquintette


**17** **SONATA FOR CLARINET AND PIANO (1960)**

*Unpublished*
*Duration:*
15 minutes
*Three movements*
*First performance:*
1960; Vienna, Austria; Erich Kaufmann, clarinet; Constance
Knox, piano


**18** **SONATINA FOR PIANO (1956)**

*Dedication:*
To composer's mother
*Unpublished*
*Duration:*
16 minutes
*Three movements*
*First performance:*
1956; Bloomington, Indiana; Indiana University; Jasper Patton, piano

**19   STRING QUARTET (1956)**

>*Dedication:*
>>To Mr. & Mrs. Melville Bryant
>
>*To be published by Southern Music Publishing Co., New York*
>*Duration:*
>>15 minutes
>
>*Three movements*
>*First performance:*
>>1957; Bloomington, Indiana; Indiana University; Berkshire Quartet

**TEN CONCERT PIECES FOR BEGINNING STRING PLAYERS.** *See* **CONCERT PIECES FOR BEGINNING STRING PLAYERS, TEN**

**20   VARIATIONS FOR WOODWIND TRIO (1955)**
For flute, B$^\flat$ clarinet, and bassoon

>*Unpublished*
>*Duration:*
>>8 minutes
>
>*Theme and six variations*
>*First performance:*
>>1956; Bloomington, Indiana; Indiana University Woodwind Trio

*James Furman*

## JAMES FURMAN
*b. Louisville, Kentucky, January 23, 1937*

Furman's early training in piano was with his aunt, Permelia Hansbrough. He
received both his Bachelor of Music Education degree (1958) and his Master of
Music degree (1965) from the University of Louisville. During his studies, he
concentrated on the study of piano, voice, theory, and composition, the latter
with George Perle. From 1962 to 1964, on a fellowship at Brandeis University,
he studied theory and composition with Irving Fine, Arthur Berger, and Harold
Shapero and was Assistant Choral Conductor. In the summer of 1966, following
his Master of Music degree, he did postgraduate work in early music and choral
literature at Harvard University.

Furman's first professional position was with the Louisville Public Schools in
1958 as music instructor. In 1964-1965 he had a similar position in the
Mamaroneck, New York Schools. During the period 1953 to 1965, he held
several organist and choir director positions. In 1965, Furman joined the faculty
of Western Connecticut State College at Danbury as Assistant Professor of Music
and in 1976 became Associate Professor. He teaches choral conducting, theory,
composition, and directs the orchestra.

Furman has appeared in numerous places as a conductor—on many occasions
conducting his own works. In New York City's Town Hall, he made his
conducting debut in May 1967. For Desto Records in 1970 he was the conductor
for a recording of the music of Richard Moryl. In addition, he was the choral
director for the BBC's documentary film on Charles Ives and prepared the chorus
for Leonard Bernstein and the American Symphony Orchestra for the July 4,
1974 Ives Centennial Concert in Danbury, Connecticut.

Already as a high school student, Furman was awarded first place in the Louisville Philharmonic Society's Young Artist's Contest and appeared with the Symphony in 1953 as pianist. As chairman of Western Connecticut State College's Twentieth Century Arts Festival, he received an Award of Merit in 1965-1966 for his distinguished service to music, conferred upon him by the National Federation of Music Clubs. An additional honor in 1967 was awarded him for his contributions to American music.

Furman is writing a book entitled *Afro-American Gospel Music* which will present the history and performance practice of gospel music. He is a member of ASCAP, the American Association of University Professors, American Federation of Teachers, Phi Mu Alpha, Phi Delta Kappa, and the Society of Black Composers.

*Sources:*
    Information submitted by composer
    An
    Gardner, Effie Tyler. *An Analysis of the Technique and Style of Selected Black-American Composers of Contemporary Choral Music*, dissertation, Michigan State University, 1979
    Kay, Ernest, editor. *Dictionary of International Biography*, Cambridge, England, International Biographical Centre, 1979, vol. 15
    Who-A
    *Who's Who In Connecticut*

1   **AVE MARIA (1971)**
Motet for chorus (SATB), unaccompanied

> *Unpublished* (IU)
> *Duration:*
>> 2 minutes
> *First performance:*
>> December 21, 1971; Frankfort, Kentucky; Bradford Hall
>> Auditorium; Kentucky State University Choir; composer,
>> conductor

2   **A BABE IS BORN IN BETHLEHEM (PUER NATUS) (1978)**
For chorus (SSATB), unaccompanied

> *Text:*
>> 14th century Latin, translated by Philip Schaff, 1869
> *Unpublished*
> *Duration:*
>> 1 minute 30 seconds

3   **BATTLE SCENES (1976)**
Suite for winds, percussion, and amplified harpsichord (or piano)

> *Unpublished*
> *Duration:*
>> 12 minutes
> *Contents*
>> 1. The Battle
>> 2. Annette
>> 3. Battle of New Orleans
>> 4. Johnson's March
> *First performance:*
>> December 19, 1976; Danbury, Connecticut; First Congregational
>> Church; West Connecticut State College Orchestra

4   **BORN IN A MANGER (1978)**
For chorus (SATB), unaccompanied

> *Text:*
>> By composer
> *Unpublished*
> *Duration:*
>> 2 minutes

**5  BYE, BYE, LULLY, LULLAY (1978)**
For chorus (SATB), solo voice (medium), unaccompanied

> *Text:*
>> 15th century English
>
> *Unpublished*
> *Duration:*
>> 1 minute 45 seconds

**6  CANTILENA FOR STRINGS (1976)**
From *Declaration of Independence*

> *Duration:*
>> 3 minutes 50 seconds

**6.1  COME THOU LONG EXPECTED JESUS (1971)**
Motet for chorus (SATB), unaccompanied

> *Text:*
>> By Charles Wesley
>
> *Dedication:*
>> "In loving memory of sister, Catherine"
>
> *Publication:*
>> New York: Lawson-Gould, 1979; Unpublished (IU)
>
> *Duration:*
>> 1 minute 40 seconds
>
> *First performance:*
>> December 12, 1971; Frankfort, Kentucky; Bradford Hall Auditorium;
>> Kentucky State University Choir; composer, conductor
>
> *Recording:*
>> The Classics Record Library 10-5573

**6.2  CONCERTO FOR CHAMBER ORCHESTRA (1964)**

> *Unpublished (piano score only, available)*
> *Duration:*
>> 9 minutes
>
> *Notes:*
>> 12-tone composition
>> To be orchestrated

**7  THE DECLARATION OF INDEPENDENCE FOR NARRATOR AND ORCHESTRA (1976)**

> *Unpublished*
> *Duration:*
>> 15 minutes

*First performance:*

> April 28, 1977; Danbury, Connecticut; Ives Concert Hall;
> Governor Ella Grasso, narrator; Western Connecticut State
> College Orchestra; composer, conductor

*Notes:*

> Orchestration includes bagpipes and optional organ
> Premiere broadcast over Voice of America, May 1977
> Review in: *The News-Times* (Danbury, Connecticut), April 29, 1977

**8  FANFARE AND FINALE FOR BRASS AND PERCUSSION (1976)**

From *Declaration of Independence*
For 3 horns, 3 trumpets, 4 trombones, 1 tuba, percussion

> *Duration:*
> 1 minute 25 seconds

**9  FANTASIA AND CHORALE FOR STRINGS (1971)**

From *I Have a Dream*

> *Duration:*
> 5 minutes 20 seconds

**10  FOR THANKSGIVING (REJOICE, GIVE THANKS AND SING) (1978)**

Anthem for chorus (SATB) with organ or piano, or unaccompanied

> *Text:*
> By Edward Plumtre
> *Unpublished*
> *Duration:*
> 2 minutes

**11  FOUR LITTLE FOXES (1962)**

For chorus (SATB) with soprano and alto solos, unaccompanied

> *Text:*
> By Lew Sarett
> *Dedication:*
> "In loving memory of my Aunt Permelia Hansbrough"
> *Publication:*
> New York: Oxford University Press, 1971 (IU)
> *Duration:*
> 4 minutes 15 seconds
> *Contents:*
> 1. Speak Lightly
> 2. Walk Softly

3. Go Lightly
4. Step Softly

*First performance:*
> December 14, 1965; Danbury, Connecticut; Western Connecticut State College Concert Choir; composer, conductor

**12   GLORY TO GOD IN THE HIGHEST (1978)**

For chorus (SATB), unaccompanied

*Text:*
> Bible, New Testament

*Dedication:*
> To Gregg Smith

*Publication:*
> New York: Lawson-Gould, 1979

*Duration:*
> 2 minutes 50 seconds

**13   GO TELL IT ON THE MOUNTAIN (1971)**

Gospel anthem for chorus (SATB), soprano and alto solos, with piano, or brass ensemble, percussion, piano, organ, and electric bass

*Text:*
> Spiritual

*Commissioned:*
> By Carl Smith

*Publication:*
> New York: Sam Fox, 1972 (piano-vocal score; parts on rental) (IU)

*Duration:*
> 3 minutes

*First performance:*
> December 12, 1971; Frankfort, Kentucky; Bradford Hall Auditorium; Kentucky State University Choir; composer, conductor

**14   HEHLEHLOOYUH—A JOYFUL EXPRESSION (1976)**

For chorus (SATB), unaccompanied

*Dedication:*
> "to my mother, Ollie Furman"

*Publication:*
> Chapel Hill, North Carolina; Hinshaw Music, 1978

*Duration:*
> 2 minutes 30 seconds

*First performance:*

> December 3, 1976; Danbury, Connecticut; First Congregational Church; Western Connecticut State College Chorus; composer, conductor

**15    HOLD ON (1972)**

Gospel anthem for chorus (SATB), solo voice, piano, and electric organ

*Text:*

> Spiritual

*Publication:*

> New York: Lawson-Gould, 1979 (IU: unpublished score)

*Duration:*

> 3 minutes

*First performance:*

> March 4, 1973; Louisville, Kentucky; Kentucky State University Choir; Carl Smith, conductor

**16    I HAVE A DREAM (1970; revised 1971)**

Oratorio for chorus (SATB), gospel chorus, baritone, folk and gospel solos, orchestra, gospel piano, organ, guitar, banjo, combo organ, electric bass, electric guitar, and drum set

*Text:*

> Writings and statements by Martin Luther King, Jr.

*Dedication:*

> "to the beloved memory of my friend, Martin Luther King, Jr."

*Commissioned:*

> By the Greenwich Choral Society

*Unpublished* (IU: score)

*Duration:*

> 40 minutes

*Contents:*

> Part I:  In the River of Life
> Part II: I Have a Dream
> Part III: Let Freedom Ring

*First performances:*

> (Original version) April 19, 1970; Greenwich, Connecticut; Greenwich Choral Society; composer, conductor
> (Revised version) January 22, 23, 24, 1971; Cincinnati, Ohio; Cincinnati Symphony Orchestra; Baroque Choral Ensemble; Central State University Chorus; Kentucky State College Chapel Choir; Wilberforce University Choir; Erich Kunzel, conductor

*Recording:*
> Premiere recorded by Recorded Publications Co., Camden, New Jersey
> (available from composer)

*Notes:*
> Reviews in: *The News-Times* (Danbury, Connecticut), April 23, 1976
> *Greenwich Times* (Connecticut), April 20, 1970

**17    I HAVE A FRIEND IN JESUS (1978)**
For voice (medium) and piano (organ)

> *Text:*
> > By composer
> *Unpublished*
> *Duration:*
> > 2 minutes

**18    I KEEP JOURNEYIN' ON (1972)**
Gospel anthem for chorus (SATB), solo voice, and piano

> *Text:*
> > By composer
> *Dedication:*
> > To Carl Smith and the Kentucky State University Choir
> *Unpublished*
> *Duration:*
> > 4 minutes
> *First performance:*
> > 1972; tour of Kentucky State University Choir; Carl Smith, conductor

**19    INCANTATION FOR CLARINET (B$^\flat$) AND STRINGS (1976)**

> *Unpublished*
> *Duration:*
> > 5 minutes
> *Notes:*
> > A recasting of the third movement of the *Suite For Solo Clarinet*
> > Also version for clarinet and piano

**20    JUPITER SHALL EMERGE (1978)**
For chorus (SSAATTBB), unaccompanied

> *Text:*
> > By Walt Whitman

*Unpublished*
*Duration:*
> 7 minutes 40 seconds

*Two sections;*
> On the Beach at Night
> Jupiter Shall Emerge

**21   LET US BREAK BREAD TOGETHER (1957)**
For chorus (SATB), unaccompanied

> *Text:*
> > Spiritual
> *Unpublished*
> *Duration:*
> > 3 minutes
> *First performance:*
> > 1958; Louisville, Kentucky; Chorals-Harmonieux Community
> > Chorus; composer, conductor

**22   MASS (1974–**
For chorus (SATB), boys' choir, soprano, alto, tenor, and bass solos, and orchestra

> *Work in progress*

**23   MUSIC FOR SAXOPHONE AND PIANO (1979)**

> *Commissioned:*
> > By Philip DeLibero
> *Work in progress*

**24   THE QUIET LIFE (1968)**
Madrigals for chorus (SATB), soprano, alto, tenor, and bass solos, unaccompanied

> *Text:*
> > Based on poems by Alexander Pope
> *Publication:*
> > (nos. 2 and 3): New York: Lawson-Gould, 1979 (IU: unpublished
> > score)
> *Durations:*
> > no. 1: 1 minute 45 seconds; nos. 2, 3, 4: each 1 minute 15 seconds
> *Contents:*
> 1. Fanfare and Pastorale (Dedicated to Claude Almand)
> 2. Quiet by Day (Dedicated to Irving Fine)
> 3. Sound Sleep by Night (Dedicated to Arthur Berger)
> 4. Thus Let Me Live (Dedicated to Leonard Kobrick)

*First performance:*
> December 16, 1969; Danbury, Connecticut; Ives Concert Hall;
> Western Connecticut State College Concert Choir; composer,
> conductor

**25   RECITATIVE AND ARIA FOR SOLO HORN AND WOODWINDS (1976)**

> *Unpublished*
> *Duration:*
>> 5 minutes 40 seconds
> *First performance:*
>> February 11, 1977; Danbury, Connecticut; Ives Concert Hall;
>> Lawrence Huntley, French horn
> *Note:*
>> Also arranged for horn and piano

**26   RESPONSES FOR CHURCH SERVICE, THREE (1978)**
For chorus (SATB), unaccompanied

> *Unpublished*
> *Contents:*
>> 1. Bless Thou the Gifts (text by Samuel Longfellow)
>> 2. The Lord Bless Thee and Keep Thee (text: Bible, Old Testament, Numbers 6:24-26)
>> 3. Amen

**27   RISE UP SHEPHERD AND FOLLOW (1977)**
For chorus (SATB) with solo voice, unaccompanied

> *Text:*
>> Spiritual
> *Duration:*
>> 1 minute 25 seconds

**28   ROULADE FOR SOLO FLUTE (1975)**

> *Dedication:*
>> To the memory of Don Wells
> *Unpublished*
> *Duration:*
>> 1 minute 50 seconds
> *Note:*
>> Written for Michael Mennone

**29**  **SALVE REGINA (1966)**
Motet for chorus (SATB), unaccompanied

> *Unpublished*
> *Duration:*
>> 2 minutes 35 seconds
>
> *First performance:*
>> December 10, 1968; Danbury, Connecticut; Berkshire Auditorium;
>> Western Connecticut State College Concert Choir; composer,
>> conductor

**30**  **SOME GLORIOUS DAY (1971)**
Gospel anthem for chorus (SATB), alto solo, and piano (electric organ)

> *Text:*
>> By composer
>
> *Publication:*
>> New York: Sam Fox, 1972 (IU)
>
> *Duration:*
>> 2 minutes 45 seconds
>
> *First performance:*
>> March 4, 1973; Louisville, Kentucky; Kentucky State University
>> Choir; Carl Smith, conductor

**31**  **SOMEBODY'S KNOCKIN' AT YOUR DOOR (1956)**
For chorus (SATB), unaccompanied

> *Text:*
>> Spiritual
>
> *Unpublished*
> *Duration:*
>> 2 minutes
>
> *First performance:*
>> 1956; Louisville, Kentucky; University of Louisville Chorus;
>> Walter Dahlin, conductor

**32**  **SONATA FOR SOLO VIOLIN (1977)**

> *Unpublished*
> *Duration:*
>> 20 minutes 40 seconds

**33** **SONGS OF JUVENILIA (1956; revised 1979)**
For voice (high) and piano (1956); for chorus (SATB) and piano or wind ensemble:
2 flutes, 2 clarinets, 2 bassoons, 2 trumpets

*Text:*
Nursery Rhymes: Tom, Tom, the Piper's Son
Little Boy Blue
Contrary Mary
Humpty Dumpty

*Unpublished*
*Duration:*
4 minutes 50 seconds
*First performance:*
1956; Louisville, Kentucky; Annette Offutte, soprano; composer,
piano

**34** **SUITE FOR SOLO CLARINET (1976)**

*Unpublished*
*Duration:*
10 minutes 10 seconds
*Four movements:*
Introitus
Moresca
Incantation
Motore Music
*First performance:*
March 5, 1976; Danbury, Connecticut; Ives Concert Hall;
Vincent Krulak, clarinet

**35** **THIS TRAIN (1970)**
For chorus (SATB), unaccompanied

*Text:*
Spiritual
*Unpublished*
*Duration:*
1 minute 30 seconds

**THREE RESPONSES FOR CHURCH SERVICE.** *See* **RESPONSES FOR
CHURCH SERVICE, THREE**

36   **THE THREEFOLD BIRTH (1962)**
Anthem for chorus (SATB), boys' voices, and organ

> *Text:*
>> Anonymous Flemish carol
>
> *Commissioned:*
>> By Church of Christ, Bedford, Massachusetts
>
> *Unpublished*
>
> *Duration:*
>> 3 minutes 30 seconds
>
> *First performance:*
>> December 1962; Beford, Massachusetts; Church of Christ;
>> church choir and organist-director

37   **TRAMPIN' (1959)**
For chorus (SATB), solo voice (medium), unaccompanied

> *Text:*
>> Spiritual
>
> *Unpublished*
>
> *Duration:*
>> 1 minute 35 seconds

38   **VALSE ROMANTIQUE (1976)**
For voice and piano

> *Unpublished*
>
> *Duration:*
>> 2 minutes 45 seconds

39   **VARIANTS (1963)**
For violin, cello, and prepared piano with assisting piano technician

> *Unpublished* (IU: score)
>
> *Duration:*
>> 9 minutes
>
> *In two parts, untitled*
>
> *First performance:*
>> Spring 1963; Waltham, Massachusetts; Brandeis University
>
> *Notes:*
>> 12-tone composition
>> Won the 1964 Brookline Library Music Composition Competition

*Adolphus Hailstork*

## ADOLPHUS CUNNINGHAM HAILSTORK
### b. Rochester, New York, April 17, 1941

On graduating from Albany High School in New York, Hailstork entered Howard University, earning his Bachelor of Music degree *Magna Cum Laude* in 1963 with a major in theory. In 1965 he earned a second Bachelor of Music and in 1966 a Master of Music degree, both in composition at the Manhattan School of Music. In 1971 he received a Ph.D. in composition from Michigan State University. During the periods between his Master's degree and the start of his work in East Lansing, he served two years as Captain in the U. S. Army, active in western Germany.

His early musical training was in violin, piano, and organ, but he subsequently pursued the piano. His initial essays in composition were for chorus and orchestra and were performed under his baton while he was still in high school. Two of his musical shows were produced in 1962 and 1963. During the same years, the National Symphony Orchestra read works which he had written while a student at Howard University. In 1963 he was appointed assistant conductor of the Howard University Chorus and won the Lucy E. Moten Travel Fellowship which enabled him to go to France and study with Nadia Boulanger. His composition *Statement, Variations, and Fugue* for orchestra written for his Master's degree was performed both by the Baltimore Symphony in 1966 and the Atlanta Symphony in 1968. While engaged in doctoral study, he served as conductor of the Michigan State University Male Chorus. In 1970-1971 he was awarded a teaching fellowship in the federally sponsored Triple T inner city project. For this he conducted and wrote music for high school bands and choral groups. In the summer of 1972, Hailstork was one of twenty-five participants selected nationally

*149*

to attend an Electronic Music Institute in New Hampshire. In June of 1978, he participated in a seminar on American music education at SUNY in Buffalo. In 1971 Hailstork joined the faculty of Youngstown State University as Assistant Professor of Music where, in 1976, he became Associate Professor. He also directed the Youngstown Playhouse and conducted the Afro-American Chorale. In 1977 he became Composer-in-Residence at Norfolk State College in Norfolk, Virginia where he teaches composition and theory.

A member of ASCAP, Hailstork credits the late Thor Johnson for being largely responsible for his success.

*Sources:*

Information submitted by composer
An

**1  AMERICAN LANDSCAPE NO. 1 (1977)**
For band

> *Commissioned:*
>> By Boardman, Ohio High School band
>
> *Duration:*
>> 9 minutes
>
> *First performance:*
>> 1977; Boardman High School band; composer, conductor
>
> *Note:*
>> Tape available from composer

**2  AMERICAN LANDSCAPE NO. 2 (1978)**
For violin and cello

> *Duration:*
>> 20 minutes
>
> *First performance:*
>> April 1978; Norfolk, Virginia; Unitarian Church
>
> *Note:*
>> Tape available from composer

**3  ANDANTE (1967)**
For organ

> *Duration:*
>> 3 minutes

**4  BAGATELLES FOR BRASS (1973)**
For brass quartet: 2 trumpets, 2 trombones

> *Publication:*
>> Illinois: Fema Publications, 1977; manuscript score (IU)
>
> *Duration:*
>> 7 minutes
>
> *First performance:*
>> Spring 1973; Youngstown, Ohio; Youngstown State University
>
> *Note:*
>> A teaching work

**5   THE BATTLE (1971)**
For men's (TTBB) chorus, unaccompanied

> *Text:*
>> By Harriet Tubman
>
> *Duration:*
>> 2 minutes
>
> *First performance:*
>> East Lansing, Michigan; Michigan State University; Men's Glee
>> Club; Robert Harris, conductor
>
> *Note:*
>> Tape available from composer


**6   BELLEVUE (1974)**
For orchestra

> *Commissioned:*
>> By the Southern Baptists' Convention
>
> *Duration:*
>> 4 minutes
>
> *First performance:*
>> March 1975; Nashville, Tennessee; Nashville Symphony
>
> *Notes:*
>> A prelude on the hymn tune "Bellevue"
>> Tape of first performance available from composer


**7   CANTO CARCELERA (1978)**
For oboe and guitar

> *Duration:*
>> 4 minutes


**8   CAPRICCIO FOR A DEPARTED BROTHER: SCOTT JOPLIN (1869-1917)**
**(1969)**
For string orchestra

> *Dedication:*
>> To Scott Joplin
>
> *Manuscript score* (IU)
> *Duration:*
>> 6 minutes

9   **CELEBRATION (1974)**
For orchestra

> *Commissioned:*
> > By J. C. Penney for a bicentennial composition for orchestra
> *Printed in New York under the auspices of J. C. Penney, 1975*
> *Duration:*
> > 3 minutes 30 seconds
> *First performance:*
> > May 1975; Minneapolis, Minnesota; Minnesota Orchestra;
> > Paul Freeman, conductor
> *Recording:*
> > Columbia M-34556 (1978)
> *Notes:*
> > Band transcription available from composer
> > Review in: *New York Times*, September 3, 1977 (New York
> > Philharmonic performance)

10   **A CHARM AT PARTING (1969)**
Song cycle (mezzo-soprano) and piano

> *Texts:*
> > By Stephen Schipachev, Alexander Pushkin, Waring Cuney, and
> > Mary Phelps
> *Publication:*
> > Nos. 2 and 4 published in: Patterson, Willis C. *Anthology of Art
> > Songs by Black American Composers*, New York: Marks, 1971;
> > manuscript score (IU)
> *Duration:*
> > 10 minutes
> *Contents:*
> > 1. Call This Whatever Name (Schipachev)
> > 2. I Loved You (Pushkin)
> > 3. Finis (Cuney)
> > 4. A Charm at Parting (Phelps)
> *First performance:*
> > Spring 1970; East Lansing, Michigan; Michigan State University;
> > Susanne Maslanka, mezzo-soprano

11   **CONCERTO FOR VIOLIN, HORN, AND ORCHESTRA (1975)**

> *Dedication:*
> > To Carol Clark

*Duration:*

15 minutes

*First performance:*

Youngstown, Ohio; Youngstown High School orchestra, composer, conductor

*Note:*

Tape for first performance available from composer

**12 DUO FOR TUBA AND PIANO (1973)**

*Dedication:*

To John Turk

*Publication:*

Illinois: Fema Publications, 1977; manuscript score (IU)

*Duration:*

7 minutes

*First performance:*

November 29, 1975; New York City; Carnegie Hall; John Turk, tuba; Dolores Fitzer, piano

**13 ELEGY AND DANCE (1971)**

For clarinet and piano

*Duration:*

5 minutes

**14 FIVE FRIENDS (1977)**

Suite for piano

*Duration:*

5 minutes

*Contents:*

Names of friends as titles

**15 FROM THE DARK SIDE OF THE SUN (1971)**

For flutes, alto flute, soprano saxophone, marimbas, vibraphones, glockenspiel, celeste, triangles, bongo drums, and strings

*Duration:*

12 minutes

*Note:*

Ph.D dissertation; abstract in *Dissertation Abstracts*, Section A, 32:3350, December 1971

**16  GUEST SUITE (1977)**
For piano, 4 hands

> *Duration:*
>> 3 minutes
>
> *Three movements, untitled*


**17  I HAVE NO LIFE BUT THIS (1966)**
For voice (soprano) and piano

> *Text:*
>> By Emily Dickinson
>
> *Duration:*
>> 2 minutes


**18  IF WE MUST DIE (1978)**
For voice (baritone) and piano

> *Text:*
>> By Claude McKay
>
> *Duration:*
>> 4 minutes


**19  IGNIS FATUUS (1976)**
For piano

> *Duration:*
>> 8 minutes
>
> *First performance:*
>> 1976; Youngstown, Ohio; Youngstown State University;
>> James Wideman, piano
>
> *Note:*
>> Tape available from composer


**20  IN MEMORIAM, LANGSTON HUGHES (1967)**
For chorus (SATB), unaccompanied

> *Text:*
>> By Edwin Markham
>
> *Dedication:*
>> To Langston Hughes
>
> *Manuscript score* (IU)

*Duration:*
> 3 minutes

*First performance:*
> 1970; East Lansing, Michigan; Michigan State University Concert Chorus

*Note:*
> Tape of first performance available from composer


**21    LAMENT FOR THE CHILDREN OF BIAFRA (1969)**
For voice with jazz ensemble, narrator, and percussion

*Duration:*
> 7 minutes

*First performance:*
> 1971; East Lansing, Michigan; Michigan State University Jazz Ensemble


**22    MADRIGALS, TWO (1968)**
For chorus (SATB), unaccompanied

*Publication:*
> New York: Piedmont Music, 1977; manuscript score (IU)

*Duration:*
> 5 minutes

*Contents:*
1. Cease Sorrows Now
2. The Silver Swan

*First performance:*
> Spring 1971; East Lansing, Michigan; Eastern High School

*Notes:*
> Tape of No. 1 available from composer
> Should be performed as a unit


**23    MOURN NOT THE DEAD (1969)**
For chorus (SATB), unaccompanied

*Text:*
> By Ralph Chaplin

*Dedication:*
> To the Michigan State Singers

*Manuscript score* (IU)

*Duration:*

    5 minutes

*First performance:*

    Spring 1971; East Lansing, Michigan; Michigan State Singers

*Notes:*

    Won Ernest Bloch Co-Award in 1970-1971

    Tape of first performance available from composer

**24   MY NAME IS TOIL (1972)**

For chorus (SATB), brass ensemble, and percussion

*Text:*

    By Adolphus Hailstork

*Manuscript score* (IU)

*Contents:*

    1. Pulse (percussion)

    2. Intrata (brass)

    3. Choral Hymn (chorus and brass)

*First performance:*

    June 11, 1972; Detroit, Michigan; St. Cecilia Church; Wayne State
        University Choral Union; Detroit Community Music School
        Percussion Ensemble; Malcolm Johns, conductor

*Notes:*

    No. 1 can be performed separately

    Nos. 2, 3 can be performed as a unit

**25   ORACLE (1977)**

For 3 flutes, 2 percussion instruments, women's voices, tenor solo, and tape

*Text:*

    Tu Fu (Chinese poet, 8th century)

*Duration:*

    8 minutes

*First performance:*

    April 1977; Youngstown, Ohio; Youngstown State University;
        student ensemble

*Note:*

    Tape available from composer

**26   OUT OF THE DEPTHS (1974)**

For symphonic band

*Dedication:*

    To the Youngstown State University Symphonic Wind Ensemble

*Publication:*
Score and parts on rental by Belwin-Mills
*Duration:*
15 minutes
*First performance:*
May 1974; Youngstown, Ohio; Youngstown State University Band;
Robert Fleming, conductor
*Note:*
1977 winner of Max Winkler Award of the College Band Directors
National Association

**27    PHAEDRA (1966)**
Tone poem for orchestra

*Duration:*
10 minutes

**28    PIANO FANTASY (1966)**

*Manuscript score* (IU)
*Duration:*
10 minutes

**29    PIANO RHAPSODY (1967)**

*Manuscript score* (IU)
*Duration:*
15 minutes
*First performance:*
Fall 1971; Columbus, Ohio; Ohio State University; Judy Darling,
piano

**30    PIANO SONATA (1978)**

*Duration:*
30 minutes
*Four movements, untitled*

**31    PIECES OF EIGHT (1972)**
For piano

*Manuscript score* (IU)

*Contents:*
1. Andantino
2. Prelude
3. Vivace
4. Prelude
5. Intermezzo
6. Campanella
7. Dance of the Elf

*Note:*
> A teaching collection; not performance material

**32    PRELUDE (1967)**
For organ

> *Manuscript score* (IU)
> *Duration:*
> > 3 minutes

**33    PROCESSIONAL AND RECESSIONAL (1977)**
For 2 trumpets, trombone, and French Horn

> *Duration:*
> > 5 minutes

**34    PULSE (1974)**
For percussion ensemble

> *Duration:*
> > 5 minutes
> *First performance:*
> > Spring 1974; Detroit, Michigan, church
> *Notes:*
> > Written as a lead-in to *My Name is Toil*
> > Tape available from composer

**35    THE RACE FOR SPACE (1963)**
A musical for chorus (SATB), 2 solo sopranos, 2 solo tenors, speaking parts, piano, and dancers

> *Text:*
> > By Dorothy Rudd Moore and Adolphus Hailstork

*Manuscript score* (IU)
*Duration:*
　　2 hours
*First performance:*
　　Spring 1963; Washington, D.C.; Howard University


**36　A ROMEO AND JULIET FANTASY (1979)**
For piano trio

　　*Duration:*
　　　7 minutes


**37　SA-1 (1971)**
For jazz ensemble

　　*Duration:*
　　　6 minutes
　　*First performance:*
　　　Spring 1971; East Lansing, Michigan; Michigan State University;
　　　Michigan State University Jazz Ensemble


**38　SCHERZO (1975)**
For percussion soloist and wind instruments: 2 flutes, 2 clarinets, 2 trumpets,
and 2 trombones

　　*Commissioned:*
　　　By Randall Erb
　　*Duration:*
　　　8 minutes
　　*First performance:*
　　　May 1975; Youngstown, Ohio; Youngstown State University;
　　　　student ensemble; Adolphus Hailstork, conductor
　　*Note:*
　　　Tape of first performance available from composer


**39　SERENADE (1971)**
For women's chorus (SSA), soprano solo, and violin solo, and piano

　　*Texts:*
　　　By Elizabeth Barrett Browning and Walt Whitman
　　*Manuscript score* (IU)

*Duration:*
    10 minutes
*First performance:*
    Spring 1971; Lansing, Michigan; Eastern High School Girl's Chorus
*Note:*
    Tape available from composer

**40**    **SET ME AS A SEAL UPON THINE HEART (1979)**
For chorus (SATB), unaccompanied

    *Text:*
        Bible, Old Testament, Song of Songs
    *Duration:*
        5 minutes

**41**    **SEXTET FOR STRINGS (1971)**

    *Score* (IU)
    *Duration:*
        15 minutes
    *Note:*
        Ph.D dissertation; abstract in *Dissertation Abstracts,* Section A, 32:3350, December 1971

**42**    **SONATA FOR HORN AND PIANO (1966)**

    *Dedication:*
        To Sharon Moe
    *Score* (IU)
    *Duration:*
        15 minutes
    *Four movements (3rd movement titled "Soliloquy")*
    *First performance:*
        Spring 1966; New York City; Manhattan School of Music; Sharon Moe, horn

**43**    **SONATA FOR VIOLIN AND PIANO (1972)**

    *Score* (IU)
    *Duration:*
        10 minutes
    *Two movements*

**44** SONATINA (1973)
For flute and piano

*Dedication:*
To Kay Hayes
*Publication:*
Illinois: Fema Publications, 1977
*Three movements*
*First performance:*
April 1975; Youngstown, Ohio; Youngstown State University;
Kay Hayes, flute; Adolphus Hailstork, piano

SONG. *See* THE WOMAN

**45** SPARTACUS SPEAKS . . . (IF WE MUST DIE) (1970)
For men's chorus (TTBB), brass ensemble, and percussion

*Text:*
By Claude McKay
*Manuscript score* (IU)
*Duration:*
5 minutes
*First performance:*
Spring 1970; East Lansing, Michigan; Michigan State University;
Michigan State University Men's Chorus and student brass
ensemble, Adolphus Hailstork, conductor

**46** SPIRITUAL (1975)
For brass octet: 4 trumpets and 4 trombones

*Commissioned:*
By Edward Tarr
*Publication:*
Century City, California: Wimbleton
*Duration:*
9 minutes
*First performance:*
1976; European cities; Edward Tarr Brass Ensemble; April 1979;
New York City; Lincoln Center; Avery Fischer Hall; Edward Tarr
Brass Ensemble
*Note:*
Tape available from composer

**47** **STATEMENT, VARIATION, AND FUGUE (1966)**
For orchestra

> *Duration:*
>> 15 minutes
>
> *First performance:*
>> 1966; Baltimore, Maryland; Baltimore Symphony
>
> *Note:*
>> Master's thesis

**48** **SUITE (1979)**
For violin and piano

> *Duration:*
>> 10 minutes
>
> *Contents:*
>> 1. Prelude
>> 2. Tango
>> 3. Meditation
>> 4. Demonic Dance
>
> *First performance:*
>> April 8, 1979; Norfolk, Virginia; Norfolk State University

**49** **SUITE FOR ORGAN (1968)**

> *Publication:*
>> North Carolina: Hinshaw Music, 1976; manuscript score (IU)
>
> *Duration:*
>> 12 minutes
>
> *Contents:*
>> 1. Prelude
>> 2. Allegretto
>> 3. Scherzetto
>> 4. Fugue
>
> *First performance:*
>> May 1975; Youngstown, Ohio; Youngstown State University,
>> Paula Kubik, organ

**50** **TRAPEZIUM (1974)**
For viola

> *Dedication:*
>> To Cindy Evans
>
> *Duration:*
>> 3 minutes

**TWO MADRIGALS.** *See* **MADRIGALS, TWO**


**TWO WEDDING SONGS.** *See* **WEDDING SONGS, TWO**


**51** **WEDDING SONGS, TWO (1977)**
For voice (soprano) and piano (organ)

> *Text:*
>> By Adolphus Hailstork
> *Duration:*
>> 5 minutes


**52** **WHO GAZES AT THE STARS (1978)**
For organ

> *Duration:*
>> 8 minutes


**53** **THE WOMAN (1972)**
For voice (soprano) and piano

> *Text:*
>> By Glen Allen
> *Dedication:*
>> To Joyce Dismuke
> *Manuscript score* (IU: cataloged under title *Song*)
> *First performance:*
>> Spring 1974; Youngstown, Ohio; Youngstown State University;
>> Teresa Maley, soprano

*Robert A. Harris*

## ROBERT A. HARRIS
*b. Detroit, Michigan, January 9, 1938*


Harris did his undergraduate and graduate work at Wayne State University in Detroit where he received a Bachelor of Science degree in music in 1962. Continuing with his studies, he took advanced work again at Wayne State and also at Eastman School of Music in Rochester, New York where he studied composition with Bernard Rogers. In 1971, upon completion of his studies with H. Owen Reed, Harris received his Ph.D. in composition from Michigan State University in East Lansing.

Harris has held positions in the Detroit area including one with the Detroit Public School System as a vocal and choral music teacher. In addition, he has served as Minister of Music in several churches. From 1964 to 1970 he was Assistant Professor of Music Theory, Literature, and Choral Ensemble at Wayne State University, and in 1970 he joined the faculty of Michigan State University where he was Associate Professor of Composition and Director of Choral Activities. In 1977 he became Professor of Conducting and Director of Choral Organizations at Northwestern University in Evanston, Illinois. In addition to his activity as composer and teacher, Harris has performed widely as a choral conductor and as a baritone. At present he is choirmaster at Trinity Church of the North Shore in Wilmette, Illinois. His own compositions have received performances throughout the United States.

Twice, in 1971 and again in 1972, Harris was the recipient of a Rockefeller Grant for study and participation in the Aspen Choral Institute. Several times he has received commissions for works. In 1974 he was chosen to be a member of a delegation representing the American Choral Directors Association to visit Europe and the USSR.

Harris is a member of several professional and honorary music organizations such as ASCAP, Phi Mu Alpha, the American Choral Directors Association, Pi Kappa Lambda, and Phi Kappa Phi.

*Sources:*
Information submitted by composer
An
*Men of Achievement,* London, England, 1977
Wh
Who-A

*Unless otherwise indicated, works are unpublished and available from composer*

**1  ADAGIO FOR STRING ORCHESTRA (1966)**

>  *Duration:*
>> 4 minutes 30 seconds
>
>  *First performance:*
>> August 1966; Rochester, New York; Eastman Chamber Orchestra


**2  BAGATELLES FOR THREE WOODWINDS, FIVE (1963)**
For flute, clarinet, and bassoon

>  *Duration:*
>> 7 minutes 30 seconds
>
>  *First performance:*
>> November 23, 1963; Detroit, Michigan; Wayne State University;
>> Composers Exchange Festival


**3  BENEDICTION (1975)**
For chorus (SATB) and optional organ

>  *Text:*
>> Bible, Old Testamant Numbers: VI:24-26
>
>  *Duration:*
>> 1 minute 20 seconds


**4  BENEDICTUS (1968)**
Motet for women's chorus (SSAA), unaccompanied

>  *Manuscript score* (HU; IU)
>  *Duration:*
>> 3 minutes 30 seconds
>
>  *First performance:*
>> December 1968; East Lansing, Michigan; Michigan State University
>> Women's Glee Club


**5  CANTICLE: THE HUNGRY ANGELS (1978)**
For chorus (SATB) and organ (or piano)

>  *Text:*
>> By Dr. Philip L. White
>
>  *Dedication:*
>> To the Chancel Choir of Trinity Church of the North Shore,
>> Wilmette, Illinois

*Publication:*
>Urbana, Illinois: Mark Foster Music Co., 1979

*Duration:*
>4 minutes

*First performance:*
>1978; Wilmette, Illinois; Trinity Church of the North Shore


**A CANTICLE OF IMMORTALITY.** *See* **REQUIEM: A CANTICLE OF IMMORTALITY**


6   **CHILDREN'S PRAYERS, THREE (1959; revised 1966)**
For women's chorus (SSA), unaccompanied

*Text:*
>Unknown

*Commissioned:*
>By Wayne State University Women's Glee Club

*Manuscript score* (HU)

*Duration:*
>4 minutes

*First performance:*
>December 2, 1960


7   **A COLLECT FOR PEACE (1972)**
For chorus (SATB) with 2 French horns, 2 trumpets, 2 trombones, and tuba

*Text:*
>By Reverend Charles G. Adams

*Commissioned:*
>By Wayne State University Choral Union

*Duration:*
>6 minutes

*First performance:*
>February 8, 1976; East Lansing, Michigan; Michigan State
>>University Singers; composer, conductor


8   **COMMUNION SERVICE (1974)**
For unison chorus with organ

*Text:*
>Mass, in English

*Commissioned:*
> By Cathedral Church of St. Paul, Detroit, Michigan

*Dedication:*
> To the choristers of St. Paul Cathedral, Elwyn Davies, organist
> and choirmaster

*First performance:*
> February 1974; Detroit, Michigan; choristers of St. Paul Cathedral;
> Elwyn Davies, organ and director

9 **CONCERT PIECE FOR BASSOON AND CHAMBER ORCHESTRA (1965)**

*Duration:*
> 7 minutes

*First performance:*
> August 3, 1965; Rochester, New York; Eastman School of Music;
> Edgar Kirk, bassoon

10 **CONCERT PIECE FOR HORN AND ORCHESTRA (1964)**

*Duration:*
> 6 minutes

*First performance:*
> August 4, 1964; Rochester, New York; Eastman School of Music;
> Verne Reynolds, French horn

11 **CONTEMPORARY RESPONSES FOR THE CHURCH SERVICE, THIRTY-
THREE (1972)**
For chorus (SATB) with organ

*Texts:*
> By several poets and liturgical

*Unpublished* (IU)

*Note:*
> Responses for all aspects of the church service: introit, communion,
> closing, prayer, offertory, scripture reading, amen, etc.

12 **CONTRASTS FOR FOUR WINDS AND STRING ORCHESTRA (1966)**
For flute, clarinet, bassoon, and French horn with string orchestra

*Duration:*
> 5 minutes 30 seconds

**13**  FANTASIA FOR UNACCOMPANIED FLUTE (1958)

> *Duration:*
>> 4 mimutes
>
> *First performance:*
>> March 1958; Detroit, Michigan; Wayne State University

FIVE BAGAETLLES FOR THREE WOODWINDS.  *See* BAGATELLES FOR THREE WOODWINDS, FIVE

**14**  FOR THE BEAUTY OF THE EARTH (1963)
For chorus (SATB) with organ (or piano)

> *Text:*
>> By Folliott S. Pierpoint
>
> *Unpublished score* (HU; IU)
>
> *Duration:*
>> 3 minutes 30 seconds
>
> *First performance:*
>> April 19, 1964; Detroit, Michigan; Christ Church

**15**  GLORY TO GOD (1963)
For chorus (SATB), unaccompanied

> *Text:*
>> Bible, New Testament, Luke II:14
>
> *Unpublished score* (HU; IU)
>
> *Publication:*
>> Hackensack, New Jersey: European-American Music Publishers, 1975
>
> *Duration:*
>> 3 minutes 30 seconds
>
> *First performance:*
>> December 8, 1963; Detroit, Michigan; People's Baptist Church

**16**  INCIDENTAL MUSIC FOR "CALIGULA" (1970)
For oboe, clarinet, bassoon, French horn, trumpet, and piano

> *Play by Albert Camus*
>
> *Duration:*
>> 9 minutes 30 seconds

*Four movements:*
>Prelude I
>Interlude I
>Prelude II
>Interlude II

*First performance:*
>April 21, 1970; Detroit, Michigan; Wayne State University; Studio West Theater

*Note:*
>Text not included with music

## 17   INTREAT ME NOT TO LEAVE THEE (1962)

For chorus (SATB), unaccompanied

*Text:*
>Bible, Old Testament, Ruth I:16-18

*Note:*
>A motet

## 18   KYRIE AND GLORIA (1964)

For chorus (SATB), organ ad lib.

*First performance:*
>May 18, 1965; Detroit, Michigan; Wayne State University; composer, conductor

## 19   LET US BREAK BREAD TOGETHER (1967)

For chorus (SSAA) and soprano solo with flute

*Text:*
>Spiritual

*Unpublished score* (HU; IU)

*Publication:*
>Hackensack, New Jersey: Joseph Boonin, 1975

*Duration:*
>4 minutes

*Note:*
>A motet

## 0   LITURGICAL SONGS, THREE (1972-1974)

For voice and piano

*Texts:*
>Liturgical, in English

*Duration:*
>6 minutes

*Contents:*
>1. Sanctus
>2. Pater noster
>3. Agnus Dei

**21    THE LORD'S PRAYER (1966)**
For chorus (SATB) with organ

>*Duration:*
>>3 minutes 30 seconds

**22    MAY THE GRACE OF CHRIST, OUR SAVIOUR (1960)**
For chorus (SATB), unaccompanied

>*Text:*
>>By John Newton

>*Duration:*
>>3 minutes 30 seconds

>*First performance:*
>>March 26, 1960; Detroit, Michigan; Ebenezer Methodist Church;
>>composer, conductor

>*Note:*
>>A motet

**23    MISSA BREVIS FOR MIXED VOICES (1963)**
For chorus (SATB), unaccompanied

**24    MOODS FOR ORCHESTRA (1968-1969)**

>*Duration:*
>>7 minutes

>*First performance:*
>>March 4, 1969; Detroit, Michigan; Detroit Symphony Orchestra;
>>Valter Poole, conductor

**25    O COME, LET US SING UNTO THE LORD (1969)**
Anthem for chorus (SATB) with organ

>*Text:*
>>Bible, Old Testament, Psalm 95:1-3; 96:3

*Dedication:*
>To Malcolm Johns and the choir of Grosse Pointe Memorial Church

*Duration:*
>4 minutes 30 seconds

*First performance:*
>March 1970; Grosse Pointe, Michigan; Grosse Pointe Memorial
>Church Choir

## 26    O PERFECT LOVE (1960)
Motet for chorus (SATB), unaccompanied

>*Text:*
>>By Dorothy Francis Gurney

>*Duration:*
>>4 minutes

>*First performance:*
>>March 26, 1960; Detroit, Michigan; Ebenezer Methodist Church;
>>Robert Harris, conductor

## 27    PSALM 47 (1960-1961)
For women's voices and five instruments: flute, clarinet, violin, viola, and cello

>*Duration:*
>>7 minutes 30 seconds

## 28    PSALMS FOR SOPRANO, HORN, AND PIANO (1968)

>*Text:*
>>Bible, Old Testament, Psalms 34, 98, 121

>*Duration:*
>>14 minutes

>*Three pieces*

>*First performance:*
>>June 1970; Detroit, Michigan; Wayne State University; Sandra
>>Smalley, soprano; Marilyn Garst, piano; Terel Cox, French horn

## 29    REJOICE, YE PURE IN HEART (1962)
For chorus (SATB), unaccompanied

>*Text:*
>>By Reverend Edward H. Plumptre

*Manuscript score* (HU; IU)
*Duration:*
> 3 minutes
*First performance:*
> April 1969; Norfolk, Virginia; First Baptist Church; Robert Harris, conductor

**30    REQUIEM: A CANTICLE OF IMMORTALITY (1971)**
For chorus (SATB), chamber choir, soprano and baritone solos, and orchestra
*Text:*
> Biblical and by Reverend Charles G. Adams
*Dedication:*
> "In memoriam, Rusha Belle Harris"
*Duration:*
> 33 minutes
*Six movements*
*Note:*
> Ph.D dissertation, abstract in *Dissertation Abstracts,* 32:1550A, September 1971

**RESPONSES FOR THE CHURCH SERVICE.** *See* **CONTEMPORARY RESPONSES FOR THE CHURCH SERVICE, THIRTY-THREE**

**31    SONATINE FOR TWO VIOLINS (1959-1960)**
*Duration:*
> 8 minutes 30 seconds
*Three movements*
*First performance:*
> June 2, 1960; Detroit, Michigan; Wayne State University; Composers' Forum Concert

**32    STRING QUARTET NO. 1 (1960-1968)**
*Duration:*
> 13 minutes
*Three movements*
*First performance:*
> June 1968; Detroit, Michigan; Wayne State University; Faculty String Quartet

**33    A STUDY FOR FLUTE AND CLARINET (1959)**

>   *Duration:*
>       2 minutes 30 seconds

**34    TE DEUM (1962)**
For men's chorus with brass quintet

>   *Text:*
>       In English

**THIRTY-THREE CONTEMPORARY RESPONSES FOR THE CHURCH SERVICE.** *See* **CONTEMPORARY RESPONSES FOR THE CHURCH SERVICE, THIRTY-THREE**

**THREE CHILDREN'S PRAYERS.** *See* **CHILDREN'S PRAYERS, THREE**

**THREE LITURGICAL SONGS.** *See* **LITURGICAL SONGS, THREE**

**35    A WEDDING INTERCESSION (1970)**
For voice (medium-high) with organ or piano

>   *Text:*
>       By Reverend Charles G. Adams
>   *Duration:*
>       4 minutes
>   *First performance:*
>       April 4, 1970; Detroit, Michigan; Tabernacle Baptist Church

*Wendell Logan, 1979*

## WENDELL MORRIS LOGAN
*b. Thomson, Georgia, November 24, 1940*

Logan received his Master's degree in 1964 from Southern Illinois University where he studied composition with Will Botje. His Ph.D. from the University of Iowa was awarded in 1969. Composition studies were with Richard Hervig and Robert Shallenberg.

Prior to receiving his Master's degree, Logan was instructor of music at Florida A&M University. His first full-time position was at Ball State University from 1967 to 1969 where he was Assistant Professor of Theory and Composition. After a second post at Florida A&M from 1969 to 1970 as head of the theory division, Logan assumed a position as Associate Professor of Theory and Composition at Western Illinois University in 1970. Leaving there in 1973, Logan took his present position at Oberlin Conservatory as Associate Professor of African-American Music. Summers were spent at Jackson State College, Valdosta State College, and as musical director for Project Radius under the auspices of the Georgia Commission on the Arts at Georgia Southern College.

Interested in jazz, Logan serves as a free-lance arranger and performer in this area. His numerous works have received many performances. He wrote an article on John Coltrane (NUMUS–WEST, vol. 2, no. 2, 1975).

Aside from grants for degree studies, Logan was the recipient of performance awards at the Goucher College Summer Music Festival in 1964, the Dallas Composers' Conference in 1965, and the National Endowment of the Arts' Composer Librettist Program. In addition, he has received grants from the Oberlin Research Council.

Logan is a member of ASCAP.

179

*Sources:*

Information submitted by composer
An
Cl
Evans, Martha. "Junkyards Yield Music," in *Valdosta Times,*
July 6, 1970
Ja
SoM

*Unless otherwise indicated, works are unpublished and available from composer*

1   **BEATS FOR C, D, AND O (1975)**
For percussion and tape

> *Dedication:*
>> To Cannonball Adderley, Duke Ellington, and Oliver Nelson
>
> *Duration:*
>> 10 minutes
>
> *First performance:*
>> 1975; Oberlin, Ohio; Oberlin Conservatory

2   **CONCERT MUSIC FOR ORCHESTRA (1963)**

> *Duration:*
>> 10 minutes
>
> *First performance:*
>> 1965; Dallas, Texas; Dallas Symphony

3   **DREAM BOOGIE (1979)**
For voice and piano

> *Text:*
>> By Langston Hughes
>
> *Dedication:*
>> To Doris Mayes
>
> *Duration:*
>> Contains improvisational passages

4   **DUO EXCHANGES (1978)**
For clarinet and percussion

> *Commissioned:*
>> By Barnie Childs
>
> *Duration:*
>> 16 minutes
>
> *First performance:*
>> May 1979; University of Redlands, California; Philip Rehfeldt, clarinet
>
> *Recording:*
>> Orion, 1979

5   **EVOCATION (1972)**
For harmonica and tape

> *Dedication:*
>> To Maurice Wong

*Duration:*
> 8 minutes

*First performance:*
> 1972; Macomb, Illinois; Western Illinois University

**6    THE EYE OF THE SPARROW (1978)**

For flute, tenor saxophone, trumpet, double bass, piano, and drums

*Duration:*
> Contains improvisational passages

*First performance:*
> 1978; Oberlin, Ohio; Oberlin Conservatory

**FIVE PIECES FOR PIANO.** *See* **PIECES FOR PIANO, FIVE**

**7    FRAGMENTS, THREE (1969)**

For voice (soprano), clarinet, piano, and percussion

*Text:*
> By Kenneth Patchen

*Dedication:*
> To K. Knight

*Duration:*
> 12 minutes

*First performance:*
> 1974; Muncie, Indiana; Ball State University

**8    FROM HELL TO BREAKFAST (1973-1974)**

For soprano, baritone, jazz ensemble, tape, narrator, 2 actors, and 2 dancers

*Text:*
> By Charles Levendowsky

*Three movements*

**9    HUGHES SET (1978)**

For men's chorus (TTB) and percussion

*Dedication:*
> To Wendell Whalum and the Morehouse Glee Club

*Duration:*
> 12-15 minutes

*First performance:*
> 1979; Atlanta, Georgia; Morehouse Glee Club; Wendell Whalum, director

*Note:*
> Set of six pieces

**10**    **ICE AND FIRE (1975)**
Cycle of five pieces for voices (soprano and baritone) and piano

> *Text:*
>> By Mari Evans
> *Dedication:*
>> To Billie Lynn Daniel and Andrew Frierson
> *Publication:*
>> two songs in Patterson, Willis. *Anthology of Art Songs by Black
>> American Composers*, New York: Marks, 1977
> *First performance:*
>> February 18, 1975; Cleveland, Ohio; Music School Settlement;
>> Billie Lynn Daniel, soprano; Andrew Frierson, baritone
> *Notes:*
>> Reviews in: *New York Times*, March 31, 1975
>> *Cleveland Press*, February 19, 1975

**11**    **MALCOLM, MALCOLM (1974)**
For chorus (SATB) and tape

> *Text:*
>> By Wendell Logan
> *First performance:*
>> 1979; Cleveland, Ohio; Shaw High School Chorus, Rosalyn Payne,
>> conductor
> *Note:*
>> Based on phonemes of name *Malcolm*

**12**    **MARTY'S BLUES (1972)**
For jazz band

> *Dedication:*
>> "to my son"
> *Publication:*
>> Seattle, Washington: Powers Publishers, 1973
> *Duration:*
>> Improvisational piece

**13**    **MEMORIES OF . . . (1972; revised 1979)**
For chamber orchestra

> *Duration:*
>> 12 minutes
> *First performance:*
>> February 24, 1979; Oberlin, Ohio; Oberlin Conservatory

**14**    **MUSIC FOR BRASSES (1970)**
For brass quintet

> *Duration:*
>> 12 minutes
> *Three movements*
> *First performance:*
>> 1973; Atlanta, Georgia; Georgia State University Brass Ensemble

**15**    **OUTSIDE ORNETT'S HEAD (1979)**
For trumpet, guitar, vibraphone, double bass, and drums

> *Dedication:*
>> To Ornette Coleman
> *Duration:*
>> Improvisational piece

**16**    **PIECES FOR PIANO, FIVE (1978)**

> *Duration:*
>> 20 minutes
> *First performance:*
>> Oberlin, Ohio; Oberlin Conservatory; Frances Walker, piano
> *Recording:*
>> Orion, 1979

**17**    **PIECES FOR VIOLIN AND PIANO, THREE (1977)**
For violin and electronic piano

> *Dedication:*
>> To Richard Young
> *Duration:*
>> 8 minutes
> *First performance:*
>> 1977; Oberlin, Ohio; Oberlin Conservatory; Richard Young, violin;
>> Sanford Margolis, piano
> *Recording:*
>> Orion, 1979

**18**    **POLYPHONY I (1968)**
For orchestra

> *Duration:*
>> 20 minutes

*Manuscript score* (IU)
*Note:*
> Ph.D. dissertation (Dissertation Abstracts XXIX, 6, 1917-A)

**19  PROPORTIONS FOR NINE PLAYERS AND CONDUCTOR (1968)**
For flute, clarinet, B$^\flat$ trumpet, trombone, violin, cello, piano, and percussion (2 players)

> *Manuscript score* (IU)
> *Duration:*
>> 16 minutes
> *First performance:*
>> 1968; Muncie, Indiana; Ball State University; New Music Ensemble
> *Recording:*
>> Orion, 1979
> *Notes:*
>> Review in: *San Francisco Chronicle*, February 7, 1973
>> Review and analysis in: *Perspectives of New Music*, vol. 9, p. 135

**20  REQUIEM FOR CHARLIE PARKER (1978–**
For large orchestra, soloists, and jazz group

> *Work in progress*

**21  SKETCH I (1975)**
For jazz ensemble

> *Duration:*
>> Improvisational piece
> *First performance:*
>> 1975; Oberlin, Ohio; Oberlin Conservatory; Oberlin Jazz Ensemble

**22  SONG OF THE WITCHDOKTOR (1976)**
For flute, violin, piano, and percussion

> *Duration:*
>> 12 minutes
> *First performance:*
>> 1976; Oberlin, Ohio; Oberlin Conservatory

**23    SONGS OF OUR TIME (1969)**
For chorus (SATB) and instruments: flute, clarinet, bassoon, French horn, trumpet, trombone, double bass, piano, and percussion

> *Texts:*
>> By W. E. B. DuBois from "The Riddle of the Sphinx"; LeRoi Jones from "The End of Man is This Beauty"; Gwendolyn Brooks from "The Soft Man"
>
> *Dedication:*
>> To George Corwin
>
> *Manuscript score* (IU)
> *Duration:*
>> 15-20 minutes
>
> *Contents:*
>> 3 songs, untitled
>
> *First performance:*
>> 1969; Ball State University Concert Choir; George Corwin, conductor
>
> *Recording:*
>> Golden Crest S-4087
>
> *Note:*
>> Review in: *New York Times*, 1969

**24    STANZAS FOR THREE PLAYERS (1966)**
For flute, cello, and piano

> *Duration:*
>> 16 minutes
>
> *First performance:*
>> 1967; Iowa City, Iowa; Center for New Music
>
> *Note:*
>> Review in: *Daily Iowan*, 1967

**25    TEXTURES (1972)**
For piano

> *Duration:*
>> 12 minutes
>
> *First performance:*
>> 1973; Iowa City, Iowa; Center for New Music

**THREE FRAGMENTS.** *See* **FRAGMENTS, THREE**

**THREE PIECES FOR VIOLIN AND PIANO.** *See* **PIECES FOR VIOLIN AND PIANO, THREE**

26 **TO MINGUS (1979)**
For vibraphone (or other instrument capable of playing chords) and guitar

> *Dedication:*
>> To André Whatley
> *Duration:*
>> 6 minutes
> *First performance:*
>> February 24, 1979; Oberlin, Ohio; Oberlin Conservatory
> *Note:*
>> Written in memory of Charlie Mingus

27 **VARIATIONS ON A MOTIVE BY COLTRANE (1975)**
For jazz ensemble

> *Duration:*
>> 4 minutes
> *First performance:*
>> 1975; Oberlin, Ohio; Oberlin Conservatory; Oberlin Jazz Ensemble

28 **WOODWIND QUINTET (1963)**

> *Duration:*
>> 10 minutes
> *Three movements*
> *First performance:*
>> 1964; Carbondale, Illinois; Southern Illinois University; Altgeld Quintet

*Carman Moore*

## CARMAN LEROY MOORE
### b. Lorain, Ohio, October 8, 1936

Moore received his Bachelor of Music degree from Ohio State University in 1958 where he concentrated on French horn and cello, occasionally playing the horn in the Columbus, Ohio symphony. Following this, he went to New York where the Juilliard School of Music awarded him a Master of Music degree in 1966. From 1958 until 1963, he studied composition in New York with Hall Overton.

In 1967 Moore founded the first course on the history of popular music at the New School for Social Research in New York City. He has written the words for more than a dozen rock songs. His book, *Somebody's Angel Child: The Story of Bessie Smith* (New York: Thomas Y. Crowell, 1969), is a result of his interest in this field. (Reviews appear in *Down Beat,* August 6, 1970, vol. 37, p. 27; *Music Journal,* December 1970, vol. 28, p. 82). In addition, Moore has been associated with Dalton School, City University of New York, New York University, Manhattanville College, Brooklyn College, and Queens College. He was music specialist for the Harlem Education Program and a consultant in Bedford-Stuyvesant for the Center for Urban Education. In 1970 he was appointed Assistant Professor of Music History at Yale University, where he remained until 1972. In March of 1972, Moore was one of the main speakers at a Symposium on African and Afro-American Music at the University of Ghana. A 1974 grant from the New York State Council on the Arts resulted in his work, *Wildfires and Field Songs,* which was performed by the New York Philharmonic.

Moore has been the music critic for the Village Voice and is a frequent contributor of reviews and articles for the Sunday *New York Times.* Besides his numerous compositions, he has written incidental music for off-Broadway plays and writes poetry and plays. For volume 2 of the *Collected Works of Scott Joplin*, he wrote the introduction, "Notes on Treemonisha." At present he devotes his time to composing and writing. In 1977 Peer-Southern Music Publishing Co. signed an exclusive publishing agreement with him, and in 1980 Doubleday will bring out his book on aesthetics of Black music entitled, *The Growth of Black Sound in America*. He is the contributing editor for the Pipeline Series published by Silver Burdett. A member of ASCAP, he was the secretary-treasurer of the Society of Black Composers, of which he was one of its founders.

*Sources:*

    Information submitted by composer
    An
    *The Black Perspective of Music,* vol. 1, no. 1, Spring 1973
    DeR
    Publicity brochure from Thomas Y. Crowell Co., New York
    SoR
    "This Week's Most Wanted Composer: Carman Moore," in
        *New York Times*, January 19, 1975, section 2, p. 1
    Who-A

# WORKS

*All compositions are available from Peer-Southern, New York*

**1 AFRICAN TEARS (BORN AGAIN) (1971)**
For chorus, jazz ensemble, percussion (7 players), 3 actors, and dancer

> *Text:*
>> By Carman Moore, after the Ghanaian poet Kofi Awooner's "Lament"
>
> *Duration:*
>> 30 minutes
>
> *First performance:*
>> July 5, 1971; New York City; Delacorte Theater
>
> *Notes:*
>> Represents conflict in modern day Africa between Western progress and ancestral tradition.
>> Review in: *New York Times*, July 7, 1971, p. 32.

**2 BEHOLD THE LAMB OF GOD (1962)**
For voice (contralto) and piano

> *Text:*
>> By Carman Moore
>
> *Duration:*
>> 3 minutes
>
> *First performance:*
>> 1962; New York City; Judson Memorial Church

**3 BELLA DONNA (1967–**
Multimedia work

> *Work in progress*

**4 CATWALK (1966)**
Ballet for orchestra

> *Commissioned:*
>> By New York City Ballet
>
> *Unpublished score* (IU)
>
> *Duration:*
>> 15 minutes

**5 CROSS FIRE (1965)**
For piano and tape

> *Dedication:*
>> To Joseph Kalichstein

*Duration:*
> 12 minutes

*First performance:*
> May 1966; New York City; Juilliard School of Music

## 6  DAWN OF THE SOLAR AGE (1978)]
For brass, percussion, and synthesizer

*Commissioned:*
> By the Committee for Sun Day

*Duration:*
> 10 minutes

*First performance:*
> May 3, 1978; New York City; UN Rose Garden and on board the "Clearwater"

## 7  DRUM MAJOR (1969)
For trumpets, trombone, tuba, percussion (2 players), and tape

*Dedication:*
> To the memory of Martin Luther King, Jr.

*Unpublished score* (IU)

*Duration:*
> 13 minutes

*First performance:*
> February 18, 1969; New York City; Society of Black Composers Concert

*Note:*
> Uses sections of Martin Luther King's last speech

## 8  FLIGHT PIECE (1969)
For flute and piano

*Duration:*
> 7 minutes

*First performance:*
> 1969; New York City; Max Pollikoff's Music in Our Time series; Robert Cram, flute; Zita Carno, piano

## 9  FOLLOW LIGHT (1977)
For chorus (SATB), percussion, and double bass

*Text:*
> By Carman Moore

*Dedication:*

"to the memory of Texana Paige Franklin and . . . Howard Swanson"

*Duration:*

8 minutes

**10**   **FOUR MOVEMENTS FOR A FASHIONABLE FIVE-TOED DRAGON (1976)**
For orchestra, chinese instruments, and jazz quintet

*Commissioned:*

By the Hong Kong Trade Development Council

*Duration:*

55 minutes

*Contents:*

Overture, Pastorale, Urban Walk, Colors, Folk Energy

*First performance:*

February 29, 1976; Hong Kong

*Recording:*

Vanguard (limited in-house pressing)

**11**   **GOSPEL FUSE (1974)**
For gospel quartet (SSSA), soprano solo, orchestra, saxophone, piano, and electric organ

*Text:*

By Carman Moore

*Commissioned:*

By San Francisco Symphony

*Dedication:*

To the memory of Hall Overton

*Duration:*

22 minutes

*First performance:*

January 22-25, 1975; San Francisco, California; San Francisco
Symphony

*Note:*

Interview by Donal Henahan in *New York Times*, January 19, 1975;
section 2, p. 1

**12**   **THE GREAT AMERICAN NEBULA (1976)**
Oratorio for string orchestra, narrator, concert band, gospel singer, chorus, and jazz trio

*Text:*

By Carman Moore

*Commissioned:*
> By the Elyria, Ohio Bicentennial Committee

*Duration:*
> 30 minutes

*Contents:*
> The American Experiment, Soft Shoe, 17th Century, Ghost Dance, Terrestrial Revolutions, March, Home Is . . . , Outer Space and Inner Grace

*First performance:*
> May 22, 1976; Elyria, Ohio

## 13   HE WILL NOT WRANGLE (1962)

For voice (soprano) and piano

*Text:*
> Bible, New Testament, Matthew XII:19-21

*Unpublished score* (IU)

*Duration:*
> 3 minutes

*First performance:*
> 1962; New York City; Judson Memorial Church

## 14   HIT: A CONCERTO FOR PERCUSSION AND ORCHESTRA (1978)

*Commissioned:*
> By the Rochester Philharmonic Orchestra through an NEA grant

*Duration:*
> 20 minutes

*Three movements*

*First performance:*
> May 4, 1978; Rochester, New York; Eastman Theater; Rochester Philharmonic Orchestra; Isaiah Jackson, conductor

## 15   THE ILLUMINATED WORKINGMAN (1975)

For mixed woodwinds, 3 percussion instruments, 4 cellos, synthesizer tape, film, and 25 dancers

*Commissioned:*
> By Erie County Council, New York

*Duration:*
> 1 hour 20 minutes

*First performance:*
> June 19, 20, 1975; Buffalo, New York; Niagara Square; members of the Buffalo Philharmonic Orchestra

**16**  IN THE WILDERNESS (1963)
For voices (2 sopranos) and piano

> *Text:*
>> By Robert Graves
>> *Unpublished score* (IU)
>> *Duration:*
>>> 6 minutes

**17**  MEMORIES (1968)
Ballet for 11 instruments and bells

> *Commissioned:*
>> By Anna Sokolow Dance Company
>> *Duration:*
>>> 15 minutes
>> *First performance:*
>>> 1969; New York City; City Hall; Composers' Recognition Week
>>> concert

**18**  A MOVEMENT FOR STRING QUARTET (1961)

> *Unpublished score* (IU)
> *Duration:*
>> 8 minutes
> *First performance:*
>> 1963; New York City; New School for Social Research

**19**  MUSEUM PIECE (1975)
For flute, cello, and tape

> *Commissioned:*
>> By Samuel Baron and Robert Sylvester
>> *Publication:*
>> New York: Peer-Southern
>> *Duration:*
>>> 12 minutes
>> *First performance:*
>>> April 1975; New York City; Guggenheim Museum; Samuel Baron,
>>> flute; Robert Sylvester, cello
> *Note:*
>> Review in: *New York Times*, April 24, 1975, p. 42

**20**   OF HIS LADY AMONG LADIES (1966)
For voice (tenor) and piano

>*Text:*
>>By Guido Cavalcanti
>*Duration:*
>>3 minutes


**21**   QUARTET FOR SAXOPHONES AND ELECTRONIC ECHO DEVICE (1978)

>*Commissioned:*
>>By LaGuardia College, New York
>*Duration:*
>>8 minutes
>*First performance:*
>>May 1978; New York City; LaGuardia College


**22**   SARATOGA FESTIVAL OVERTURE (1966)
For orchestra

>*Commissioned:*
>>By Lincoln Kirstein, director of New York City Ballet
>*Duration:*
>>10 minutes


**23**   SEAN-SEAN (1965)
For French horn, 3 cellos, and tape

>*Commissioned:*
>>By Martha Clarke, choreographer
>*Dedication:*
>>To Sean O'Casey
>*Unpublished score* (IU)
>*Duration:*
>>10 minutes
>*First performance:*
>>1965; New York City; Juilliard School of Music
>*Note:*
>>Tape contains readings from Sean O'Casey

**24** SONATA: VARIATIONS FOR MANDOLIN AND PIANO (1965)

> *Unpublished score* (IU)
> *Duration:*
>> 9 minutes
> *First performance:*
>> 1965; New York City; New York Mandolin Society


**25** SONATA FOR PIANO (1962)

> *Publication:*
>> New York: Peer-Southern
> *Duration:*
>> 10 minutes
> *In one movement*
> *First performance:*
>> 1963; New York City; New School for Social Research
> *Recording:*
>> To be released by Phillips


**26** SONATA FOR VIOLONCELLO AND PIANO (1965)

> *Duration:*
>> 7 minutes
> *Two movements*
> *First performance:*
>> 1965; New York City; Juilliard School of Music


**27** SYMFONIA (sic) (1964)
For chamber orchestra

> *Duration:*
>> 12 minutes


**28** THEATRE MUSIC SUITE TO JoANNE (1976)
For piano, bass, saxophone, flute, electric guitar, percussion, and synthesizer

> *Duration:*
>> 30 minutes
> *First performance:*
>> October 7, 1976; New York City; Riverside Church

**29 TRYST (1964)**
For clarinet, cello, and percussion

> *Duration:*
>> 8 minutes
> *First performance:*
>> 1965; New York City; Juilliard School of Music


**30 WEDDING CANTATA (1963)**
For chorus, tenor solo, and instrumental quartet

> *Text:*
>> By Carman Moore; James Joyce, "Chamber Music"; Robert Herrick, "The Goodnight" ("Blessing")
> *Commissioned:*
>> By Peggy and Roy Watts
> *Duration:*
>> 13 minutes
> *First performance:*
>> 1963; New York City; New School for Social Research


**31 WILDFIRES AND FIELD SONGS (1974)**
For orchestra

> *Commissioned:*
>> By New York Philharmonic through a grant from the New York State Council of the Arts
> *First performance:*
>> January 23-25, 28, 1975; New York City; Lincoln Center; Avery Fischer Hall; New York Philharmonic; Pierre Boulez, conductor
> *Notes:*
>> Interview by Donal Henahan in *New York Times*, January 19, 1975, section 2, p. 1.
>> Review in: *New York Times*, January 24, 1975, p. 18.


**32 WITH THEE CONVERSING (1962)**
For voice (soprano) and piano

> *Text:*
>> By John Milton from "Paradise Lost", IV Eve to Adam

*Duration:*
> 6 minutes

*First performance:*
> New York City; New York Public Library; Composers' Forum
> Concert


**33    YOUTH IN A MERCIFUL HOUSE (1965)**

Ballet for piccolo, 2 bassoons, viola, vibraphone, and percussion: cymbals, bongo drums, snare drum, and bass drum

*Commissioned:*
> By Mary Barnett, choreographer

*Unpublished score* (IU)

*First performance:*
> 1965; New York City; Juilliard School of Music

*Recordings:*
> Desto (1975).
>
> Folkways 33902 (1976): Review in: *Stereo Review*, vol. 37, no. 3 (September 1976), pp. 126-127.

*Dorothy Moore*

## DOROTHY RUDD MOORE
*b. Wilmington, Delaware, June 4, 1940*


Moore grew up in New Castle, Delaware. She received her Bachelor of Music degree in theory and composition, *magna cum laude* from Howard University in Washington, D. C., in 1963. A Lucy Moten Fellowship permitted her to continue her studies in Paris in the summer of 1963 with Nadia Boulanger. In 1965 she was a student of Chou Wen-chung in New York City.

Moore taught theory and piano at the Harlem School of the Arts in 1965-1966. In 1969, she gave courses in music history and appreciation at New York University and Bronx Community College in 1971. She currently gives private instruction in piano and ear training.

In addition to her teaching and composing, Moore is active as a singer. An accomplished poet, Moore sets her own texts to music. Some of her poetical works have been published, and many of her compositions have received several performances. Her works for cello have been performed widely by her husband, Kermit Moore. For a studio with which she is affiliated, she frequently arranges solo songs of other composers for 2 and 3 voices.

Moore was one of the founders of the Society of Black Composers.


*Sources:*

>Information submitted by composer
>Wh
>Wi

*Works are unpublished and are available through American Composers Alliance*

**1   BAROQUE SUITE FOR UNACCOMPANIED VIOLONCELLO (1964-1965)**

> *Dedication:*
>> To Kermit Moore
>
> *Duration:*
>> 15 minutes
>
> *First performance:*
>> November 21, 1965; New York City; Harlem School of the Arts;
>> Kermit Moore, cello
>
> *Note:*
>> Review in: *The Morning News* (Wilmington, Delaware),
>> April 22, 1970

**2   DIRGE AND DELIVERANCE (1971)**
For cello and piano

> *Commissioned :*
>> By Kermit Moore
>
> *Duration:*
>> 16 minutes
>
> *Two movements:*
>> Second movement has written out cadenza
>
> *First performance:*
>> May 14, 1972; New York City; Lincoln Center; Alice Tully Hall;
>> Kermit Moore, cello; Zita Carno, piano
>
> *Notes:*
>> Must be played as a unit
>> Review in: *New York Times*, February 25, 1975

**3   DREAM AND VARIATIONS (1974)**
For piano

> *Duration:*
>> 20 minutes
>
> *First performance:*
>> February 23, 1975; New York City; Carnegie Recital Hall;
>> Zita Carno, piano
>
> *Notes:*
>> Theme and variations
>> Written for Ludwig Olshansky
>> Review in: *New York Times*, February 25, 1975

**4a    FROM THE DARK TOWER (1970)**

For voice (mezzo-soprano), cello, and piano

*Texts:*

By Black American poets: Arno Bontemps, Countee Cullen,
Waring Cuney, Langston Hughes, Georgia Douglas Johnson,
Herbert Clark Johnson, and James Weldon Johnson

*Commissioned:*

By Kermit Moore

*Duration:*

34 minutes

*Contents:*

1. O Black and Unknown Bards (J. W. Johnson)
2. Southern Mansion (Bontemps)
3. Willow Bend and Weep (H. C. Johnson)
4. Old Black Men (G. D. Johnson)
5. No Images (Cuney)
6. Dream Variation (Hughes)
7. For a Poet (Cullen)
8. From the Dark Tower (Cullen)

*First performance:*

October 8, 1970; Norfolk, Virginia; Norfolk State College;
Hilda Harris, mezzo-soprano; Kermit Moore, cello; Alan Booth,
piano

*Notes:*

Reviews in: *Music Journal*, January 1972
*New York Times*, February 25, 1975

**4b    FROM THE DARK TOWER (1972)**

For voice (mezzo-soprano) and chamber orchestra: flute, oboe, clarinet, trumpet,
percussion, 2 violins, viola, cello, and double bass

*Commissioned:*

By Hilda Harris

*Duration:*

22 minutes

*Contents:*

Four songs from earlier work (nos. 1, 3, 6, 8) orchestrated

*First performance:*

October 29, 1972; New York City; Lincoln Center; Philharmonic
Hall; Hilda Harris, mezzo-soprano; Symphony of the New World;
George Byrd, conductor

*Notes:*

>  Review in: *The Jersey Journal* (Jersey City, New Jersey),
>  October 30, 1972, p. 19.
>  *New York Times*, October 30, 1972, p. 39.

5   **IN CELEBRATION (1977)**
For chorus, soprano and baritone solos, and piano

>  *Text:*
>  A collage of poems by Langston Hughes
>  *Dedication:*
>  To Howard Swanson in honor of his 70th birthday
>  *Commissioned:*
>  By the Triad Chorale
>  *Duration:*
>  5 minutes
>  *First performance:*
>  June 12, 1977; New York City; Alice Tully Hall; The Triad Chorale;
>  Noel DaCosta, director

6   **LAMENT FOR NINE INSTRUMENTS (1969)**
For flute, oboe, clarinet, trumpet, trombone, percussion, violin, viola, and cello

>  *Unpublished work available from composer*
>  *Duration:*
>  8 minutes
>  *First performance:*
>  August 16, 1969; New York City; Studio 58; Kermit Moore, conductor
>  *Note:*
>  Written for reading session of Society of Black Composers performing
>  new works

7   **MODES FOR STRING QUARTET (1968)**

>  *Duration:*
>  12 minutes
>  *Three movements*
>  *First performance:*
>  May 28, 1968; New York City; Harlem School of the Arts; Sanford
>  Allen, violin; Selwart Clarke, violin; Alfred Brown, viola; Kermit
>  Moore, cello
>  *Note:*
>  Review in: *New York Times*, May 29, 1968 and February 25, 1975

**8** **MOODS (1969)**
For viola and cello

*Duration:*
15 minutes
*Contents:*
1. Agitated and Erratic
2. Melancholic
3. Frenetic
*First performance:*
May 20, 1969; New York City; Intermediate School no. 201;
Society of Black Composers Concert; Selwart Clarke, viola;
Kermit Moore, cello
*Notes:*
Written on a Society of Black Composers Grant
Second movement written and performed already in 1965

**9** **NIGHT FANTASY (1978)**
For clarinet and piano

*Duration:*
12 minutes
*A sonata in two movements*

**10** **PIECES FOR VIOLIN AND PIANO, THREE (1967)**

*Commissioned:*
By Richard Elias
*Duration:*
10 minutes
*Contents:*
1. Vignette
2. Episode
3. Caprice
*First performance:*
March 2, 1967; New York City; Carnegie Recital Hall; Richard
Elias, violin; David Garvey, piano
*Note:*
Review in: *New York Times*, March 7, 1967 and February 25, 1975

**11** **REFLECTIONS FOR SYMPHONIC WIND ENSEMBLE (1962)**

*Unpublished work available from composer*
*Duration:*
10 minutes

*First performance:*

    1962; Washington, D. C.; Howard University School of Fine Arts; Howard University Symphonic Wind Ensemble; William Penn, conductor

*Note:*

    Written for a contest and won

**12    SONGS (1962)**

For voice (soprano) and oboe

*Text:*

    By Rudyard Kipling from "The Rubáiyát of Omar Khayyám"

*Duration:*

    15 minutes

*First performances:*

    August 1963; Paris, France; Jeu de Paume; Janet Lytle, soprano; Sandra Fischer, oboe.

    February 23, 1975; New York City; Carnegie Recital Hall; Dorothy Moore, soprano; Harry Smyles, oboe.

*Notes:*

    Should be performed as a unit

    Review in: *Music Journal*, April 1975

**13    SONNETS ON LOVE, ROSEBUDS, AND DEATH (1976)**

For soprano, violin, and piano

*A cycle of eight songs*

*Texts:*

    By Alice Dunbar Nelson, Clarissa Scott Delany, Gwendolyn B. Bennett, Langston Hughes, Countee Cullen, Arna Bontemps, and Helen Johnson

*Commissioned:*

    By Miriam Burton and Sanford Allen

*Duration:*

    21 minutes

*Contents:*

    1. Sonnet: I had no thought of violets of late (Nelson)
    2. Joy (Delany)
    3. Sonnet: Some things are very dear to me (Bennett)
    4. Sonnet: He came in silvern armour (Bennett)
    5. Song for a Dark Girl (Hughes)

6. Idolatry (Cullen)
7. Youth Sings a Song of Rosebuds (Bontemps)
8. Invocation (Johnson)

*First performance:*
> May 23, 1976; New York City; Alice Tully Hall; Miriam Burton, soprano; Sanford Allen, violin; Kelly Wyatt, piano

**14    SYMPHONY NO. 1 (1963)**

*Available from composer*
*Duration:*
> 15 minutes

*In one movement*
*First performance:*
> May 1963; Washington, D. C.; National Symphony Orchestra

**THREE PIECES FOR VIOLIN AND PIANO.** *See* **PIECES FOR VIOLIN AND PIANO, THREE**

**15    TRIO FOR VIOLIN, CELLO, AND PIANO (1970)**

*Commissioned:*
> By The Reston Trio

*Duration:*
> 15 minutes

*Three movements*
*First performance:*
> March 26, 1970; New York City; Carnegie Recital Hall; The Reston Trio

*Note:*
> Review in: *New York Times*, March 27, 1970

**16a    THE WEARY BLUES (1972)**
For voice (baritone), cello and piano

*Text:*
> By Langston Hughes "The Weary Blues"

*Commissioned:*
> By Rawn Spearman

*Published in:*
> Patterson, Willis C. *Anthology of Art Songs By Black American Composers*, New York: Marks, 1971

*Duration:*

> 5 minutes

*First performance:*

> November 20, 1972; New York City; Horace Mann Auditorium;
> Rawn Spearman, baritone; Kermit Moore, cello; Kelley Wyatt,
> piano

**16b  THE WEARY BLUES (1979)**

For voice (baritone) and orchestra: 2 flutes, 2 oboes (English horn), 2 clarinets
(bass clarinet), 2 bassoons, 2 horns, timpani, piano, strings

*Duration:*

> 10 minutes

*First performance:*

> February 2, 1979; Buffalo, New York; Kleinhaus Hall; Benjamin
> Matthews, baritone; Buffalo Philharmonic Orchestra; Michael
> Tilson Thomas, conductor

*Note:*

> An orchestration of 1972 work

## ARRANGEMENTS

*Most of the arrangements were completed in 1972 and 1973*
*All were commissioned, and all have been performed numerous times*

**1  AVE MARIA**

Sacred song by Charles Gounod
For women's chorus (SSA) and piano

**2  CHARITY**

Song by Richard Hageman on a text by Emily Dickinson
For vocal duet (SA)

**3  DEEP RIVER**

For women's chorus or duet (SA) and piano (by Harry T. Burleigh)

> *Text:*
>
> > Spiritual

**4**  HE'S GOT THE WHOLE WORLD IN HIS HANDS (1974)
For chorus (SATB) and piano (by Margaret Bonds)

    *Text:*
      Spiritual

**5**  IF MUSIC BE THE FOOD OF LOVE
Song by Henry Purcell
For women's chorus or duet (SA) and piano

    *Unpublished score* (HU)

**6**  LET MY SONG FILL YOUR HEART
Song by Ernest Charles
For women's chorus (SSA) and piano

**7**  LULLABY (1974)
Song by Cyril Scott on a text by Christine Rossetti
For vocal duet (SS) and piano

**8**  LULLABY FROM OPERA "JOCELYN"
Opera by Benjamin Godard
For women's chorus or duet (SA) and piano

    *Unpublished score* (HU)

**9**  NYMPHS AND SHEPHERDS
Song by Henry Purcell
For women's chorus or trio (SSA) and piano (by Miles B. Foster)

**10**  ON WINGS OF SONG
Song by Felix Mendelssohn, Op. 34, no. 2
For vocal duet (SS) and piano

**11**  PASSING BY
Song by Henry Purcell
For women's chorus (SA) and piano

    *Unpublished score* (HU)

**12  RIDE ON, KING JESUS**
For chorus (SATB) and piano

> *Text:*
> > Spiritual
> *Unpublished score* (HU)


**13  THANKS BE TO THEE (1977)**
Aria by George Frederic Händel
For vocal trio (SST) and piano


**14  THIS LITTLE LIGHT OF MINE**
For chorus (SATB), unaccompanied

> *Text:*
> > Spiritual
> *Unpublished score* (HU)


**15  WIEGENLIED**
Song by Johannes Brahms, Op. 49, no. 4
For women's chorus or trio (SSA) and piano

> *Unpublished score* (HU)

*John Price*

## JOHN ELWOOD PRICE
### b. Tulsa, Oklahoma, June 21, 1935

Price is a prolific composer in all media. At the age of five, he began his piano studies and went on later to study numerous other instruments. His first composition was performed at his sixth grade graduation ceremonies. Avidly interested in music and encouraged by his family, he continued his musical education with the study of harmony and orchestration which he learned at the junior high and high school levels. Majoring in composition, Price received his Bachelor of Music degree at Lincoln University in Missouri in 1957 where he wrote the music for some of the University's theatrical productions. It was at this time that he developed a particular interest in writing music for the stage. Following his graduation, he became staff pianist, resident composer, and vocal coach for two years at the Karamu Theater in Cleveland, Ohio. There he composed incidental music for ballet and stage works in both children's and adult theaters. Two years in the Army followed before he entered Tulsa University in 1961, where he received his Master's degree in composition in 1963. A brief association with the AMS Players of Atlanta followed. With this group, he toured France and Germany as its musical director for the Defense Department. From 1964 to 1974 he was Chairman of the Fine Arts Department at Florida Memorial College with a year off (1967-1968) for studies toward the Ph.D. at Washington University in St. Louis.

Price is very active in writing music, particularly for the stage; he is also a stage director. Between 1969 and 1971 he wrote and was the MC for a Sunday evening radio program entitled "Classical Black," heard in the south Florida and Caribbean areas.

*213*

In September 1974 he joined the faculty of Eastern Illinois University at Charleston as a full-time member of the Music Theory and History Department, after having taught there during the summers of 1970 and 1971.

Price is the recipient of several awards from Florida Memorial College in 1972 and 1973 and from Alpha Phi Alpha which conferred on him the Outstanding Service Award in 1972. In 1974, along with eleven other scholars, Price was selected by the Phelps-Stokes Foundation as an exchange scholar to lecture in the Caribbean. In 1974 and 1975 he was a visiting professor in Caribbean Culture and Mayan Culture at Florida Institute of Technology. Eastern Illinois University honored him in 1979 with a Distinguished Faculty Award.

Price has done extensive research on Black music, including the life and works of Chevalier de Saint-Georges, Ignatius Sancho, and Marcus Garvey. In addition, he is active in writing poetry, short stories, and plays.

*Sources:*

Information submitted by composer

An

"The Black Musician as Artist and Entrepreneur," Phelps-Stokes Fund, 1974

"Classical Black," in *Miami Herald* (Florida), December 19, 1971

I-Who, 1976

Ja

Pan American Union. Music section. *Composers of the Americas,* Washington, D. C., vol. 19, 1977

*Personalities Caribbean,* University of the West Indies, 1976-1977

"Profile . . . Composer on the Threshold of Fame," in *The Lamp,* Miami, Florida, Florida Memorial College, 1970

*The Sphinx,* (magazine of Alpha Phi Alpha fraternity), Spring 1976, biographical article

"225 Written, 225 More to Go," in *Miami Herald* (Florida), December 19, 1971

*Unless otherwise indicated, works are unpublished and available from composer*

1  **AMENS, FIFTY-TWO (1968-1975)**
   For voices in various combinations


2  **... AND SO FAUSTUS GAINED THE WORLD AND LOST HIS SOUL or WHATEVER HAPPENED TO HUMANITY? (1976)**
   For small orchestra

> *Published in:*
> > Floyd, Sam. *An Anthology of Music by Black Contemporary Composers*, Carbondale, Illinois, Southern Illinois University
> *Duration:*
> > 14 minutes


3  **AVE MARIA (1972)**
   For chorus (SATB), unaccompanied

> *Duration:*
> > 4 minutes 12 seconds


4  **THE BALLAD OF CANDY MAN BEECHUM (1962; revised 1964)**
   Incidental music for voice and guitar; revised version for chamber orchestra
   Revised version commissioned by AMS Players of Atlanta, Georgia

> *Text:*
> > By Ray McIver
> *Duration:*
> > 1 hour
> *Songs:*
> > 1. Ain't Nothin' Like Saturday Night (and dance)
> > 2. Cat Fish
> > 3. Song With the Yella Gal
> > 4. Ballad of Candy Man Beechum
> > 5. I Work and Slave
> > 6. Candy Man's Funeral Dance and Lament


5  **BARELY TIME TO STUDY JESUS (1970; revised 1975-1976; revised 1977)**
   For chorus, unaccompanied, soloist, and seven readers; revised 1975-1976 version includes orchestra; revised 1977 version includes percussion ensemble with original version

> *Text:*
> > By Robert Chute, poem about Nat Turner

*Durations:*
>Original: 14 minutes; revised 1975-1976: 30 minutes; revised 1977: 40 minutes
>*Performed several times by the James and Rosamond Johnson Ensemble of Florida Memorial College, Miami, Florida*

**6  BEACH VERSE I FOR INSTRUMENTS (1960)**
For flute, oboe, clarinet, and bongo drums

>*Duration:*
>7 minutes

**7  BLUES AND DANCE II (1972)**
For clarinet and piano

>*Duration:*
>5 minutes 36 seconds

**8  CAROL I (1958)**
For children's choirs and piano

>*Text:*
>By John E. Price
>*Dedication:*
>To the Children's Chorus of Karamu House, Cleveland, Ohio
>*Duration:*
>3 minutes 10 seconds

**9  CAROL II (1962)**
For voice and piano

>*Duration:*
>3 minutes 46 seconds

**10  CAROL III (1970)**
For voice and piano *or* voice, female trio, chorus, and piano

>*Text:*
>By John E. Price
>*Dedication:*
>To Joyce Brown and James and Rosamond Johnson Ensemble of Florida Memorial College, Miami

*Duration:*

    6 minutes

*First performance:*

    December 1971; Miami, Florida; Florida Memorial College; James and Rosamond Johnson Ensemble

*Note:*

    "A protest against the falsity of the phrase, 'Law and Order'"

**11    CAROL IV (1972)**

For voice and piano

    *Text:*

        By John E. Price

    *Duration:*

        3 minutes 20 seconds

**12    CAROL V (1971)**

For voice (tenor) and flute

    *Text:*

        By John E. Price

    *Duration:*

        4 minutes

    *First performance:*

        Date ?; Miami, Florida; Florida Memorial College

**13    CAROL VI (1972)**

For chorus (SATB), unaccompanied

    *Text:*

        By John E. Price

    *Duration:*

        4 minutes

**14    CAROL VII (1972)**

For chorus (SATB), unaccompanied

    *Text:*

        By John E. Price

    *Duration:*

        4 minutes 15 seconds

15 **CAROL VIII (1974)**
For chorus (SATB), unaccompanied

> *Text:*
>> By John E. Price
>
> *Duration:*
>> 5 minutes 10 seconds
>
> *Note:*
>> *See* alternate version: *For Earth, For People, A Carol*

16 **CAROL IX (1974)**
For chorus (SATB) and two soloists, unaccompanied

> *Text:*
>> By John E. Price
>
> *Duration:*
>> 6 minutes

17 **CAROL X (1972)**
For chorus (SATB), unaccompanied

> *Text:*
>> By John E. Price
>
> *Duration:*
>> 8 minutes

18 **CAROL XI (1972)**
For chorus (2-part--high and low voices), unaccompanied

> *Text:*
>> By John E. Price
>
> *Duration:*
>> 4 minutes

19 **CAROLS, TWO (1973)**
For chorus (SATB), unaccompanied

> *Text:*
>> By John E. Price
>
> *Duration:*
>> 6 minutes 21 seconds

20    **CAROLS FOR CHILDREN'S CHOIR AND PIANO, SEVEN (1975-1976)**

**THE CHAIRS.** *See* **ENTR'ACTE FOR "THE CHAIRS"**

21    **CHORAL PIECE I (1957)**
For chorus (SATB), unaccompanied

> *Text:*
>> By John E. Price
>
> *Duration:*
>> 4 minutes

22    **CHORALE (1956)**
For chorus (SATB) with piano

> *Text:*
>> By John E. Price
>
> *Duration:*
>> 3 minutes

23    **CHORUSES ON POEMS BY ORALE LYNCH (1972)**
For chorus (SATB), unaccompanied

> *Duration:*
>> Various timings
>
> *Five pieces*

24    **COLLECTIONS OF POPULAR WORKS (1957-1974)**
For voice and piano

> *Texts:*
>> By John E. Price
>
> *Duration:*
>> Various timings
>
> *Note:*
>> Various moods

25    **COLLEGE SONATA (1957)**
Opera for chorus (SATB), soprano, mezzo-soprano, 2 tenors, baritone, and bass-baritone, with orchestra and band

> *Text:*
>> By John E. Price

*Duration:*
> ca. 2 hours 25 seconds

*Two acts*

*Note:*
> A science fiction story about the last football game

**26  COLUMBINE (1959)**
For voice, unaccompanied

> *Text:*
>> By Ann Flagg
>
> *Duration:*
>> Various timings
>
> *Two songs*
>
> *First performance:*
>> 1958; Cleveland, Ohio; Karamu House

**27  CONCERTO FOR PIANO AND ORCHESTRA (1969)**

> *Dedication:*
>> To Ruth Norman Bostic
>
> *Duration:*
>> 25 minutes
>
> *Three movements*

**28  CONCERTO FOR VIOLONCELLO AND ORCHESTRA (1959-1974)**

> *Duration:*
>> 27 minutes 30 seconds
>
> *Three movements:*
>> Recitative-Spiritual-Variations
>
> *Note:*
>> Written for Donald White

**29  CONFESSION (1972)**
For chorus, soloists, speakers, and orchestra

> *Text:*
>> By Nat Turner, his confession
>
> *Duration:*
>> 20 minutes
>
> *Note:*
>> Incorporated into the revised version of *Barely Time to Study Jesus*

**30**    **CYCLE OF PIECES (1972-1974)**
For men's chorus, unaccompanied

> *Text:*
>> By Juan Latino (in Latin)
>
> *Dedication:*
>> To the Morehouse Glee Club of Morehouse College, Atlanta,
>> Georgia
>
> *Duration:*
>> 36 minutes

**31**    **THE DAMNATION OF DOCTOR FAUSTUS (1962-1963)**
For chorus (SATB), tenor solo, and chamber orchestra

> *Text:*
>> By Christopher Marlowe (last scene)
>
> *Dedication:*
>> To "my mother, Aunts Robbie, Jay, and Dr. Bela Rozsa"
>
> *Duration:*
>> 33 minutes

**32**    **DANCE FOR ENGLISH HORN AND ORCHESTRA (1952)**

> *Duration:*
>> 14 minutes

**33**    **DEATH OF A SALESMAN (1958)**
Incidental music for flute and clarinet

> *Play:*
>> By Arthur Miller
>
> *First performance:*
>> 1958; Cleveland, Ohio; Karamu House

**34**    **DONA NOBIS PACEM (1972)**
For chorus (SATB), unaccompanied

> *Text:*
>> Liturgical; Latin
>
> *Duration:*
>> 4 minutes 40 seconds

35   **DUET (1959)**
For French horn and trombone

> *Duration:*
>> 5 minutes

36   **EDITORIAL I (1969)**
For orchestra

> *Duration:*
>> 16 minutes 25 seconds
>
> *Note:*
>> "A mirror in sounds after reading an editorial"

37   **EDITORIAL II (1966)**
For piano

> *Duration:*
>> 12 minutes
>
> *First performance:*
>> 1966; Lewiston, Maine; Bates College

38   **ENTR'ACTE FOR "THE CHAIRS" (1962)**
For bassoon, French horn, and piano

> *Play:*
>> By Eugéne Ionesco
>
> *Commissioned:*
>> By William McKee
>
> *First performance:*
>> 1962; Tulsa, Oklahoma

39   **EPISODE (1956-1957)**
For piano and small orchestra

> *Duration:*
>> 15 minutes 50 seconds

40   **FAIRY TALE WOOD (1959)**
Incidental music for voice and piano

> *Text:*
>> By Ann Flagg
>
> *First performance:*
>> 1959; Cleveland, Ohio; Karamu House

**41   FANFARE AND MARCH (1954)**
For 3 trumpets and organ

>*Duration:*
>>8 minutes
>
>*First performance:*
>>1955; Jefferson City, Missouri; Lincoln University


**42   FANFAYRE (1974)**
For 5 trumpets

>*Duration:*
>>3 minutes


**43   FAUSTUS VARIATIONS (1978)**
For percussion ensemble

>*Dedication:*
>>To Johnny Lane and the Eastern Illinois University Percussion
>>Ensemble
>
>*Duration:*
>>25 minutes
>
>*Thirteen variations*


**44   THE FEAST OF UNITY (1969)**
A stage review for chorus (SATB), soprano, alto, tenor, and baritone soloists,
flute, oboe, alto saxophone, tenor saxophone, 2 trumpets, 2 trombones, tuba,
piano/harp, percussion, and string octet, actors, and dancers

>*Text:*
>>By Sam White, Sharon Lockhart, and others
>
>*Duration:*
>>1 hour 27 minutes
>
>*Note:*
>>"Comments on society and possible solutions for our problems"


**FIFTEEN SPIRITUALS.** *See* **SPIRITUALS, FIFTEEN**


**FIFTY-TWO AMENS.** *See* **AMENS, FIFTY-TWO**

**45**   **FIVE AND FIVE (1978)**
For piano

> *Commissioned by and dedicated to:*
>     Mary Kogen
> *Publication:*
>     Miami, Florida: Slave Ship Press, 1979
> *Thirty-three pieces each using various five finger positions*

**FIVE PIECES.** *See* **PIECES, FIVE**

**FIVE SETS OF PIECES.** *See* **SETS OF PIECES, FIVE**

**46**   **THE FLY IN THE COFFIN (1962)**
Incidental music for unaccompanied voice

> *Text:*
>     By Erskine Caldwell, from a short story, adapted by Ray McIver
> *Commissioned:*
>     By AMS Players, Atlanta, Georgia
> *Contents:*
>     1. Ain't It Sad
>     2. Church Funeral Scene

**FOR BRASS QUARTET.** *See* **HYMN AND DEVIATION**

**47**   **FOR EARTH, FOR PEOPLE, A CAROL (1972)**
For voice (high) and piano or voice (high), unison chorus, and piano

> *Text:*
>     By John E. Price
> *Dedication:*
>     To Margaret King
> *Duration:*
>     7 minutes
> *First performance:*
>     December 1972; Miami, Florida; Florida Memorial College
> *Notes:*
>     "An ecological plea for humans to protect the earth from careless
>         destruction."
>     An alternate version of *CAROL VIII.*

**48** **FOR L'OVERTURE (1951)**
For piano and orchestra

> *Duration:*
>> 15 minutes
> *Note:*
>> "A kind of tone poem dedicated to Toussaint L'Ouverture"


**49** **FOR THREE INSTRUMENTS (1956)**
For clarinet, tuba, and piano

> *Duration:*
>> 3 minutes 23 seconds


**50** **FOR VOICE AND PIANO (1955)**
No text

> *Duration:*
>> 3 minutes


**FORSIGHT OF TIME AND THE FUTURE.** *See* **FORSIGHT OF TIME AND THE UNIVERSE**


**51** **FORSIGHT OF TIME AND THE UNIVERSE (1955)**
Monologue with clarinet, trumpet, and percussion

> *Text:*
>> By John E. Price
> *Duration:*
>> 15 minutes
> *First performance:*
>> 1955; Jefferson City, Missouri; Lincoln University
> *Note:*
>> "A science fiction scene about the creation of the universe"


**FORTY HYMNS.** *See* **HYMNS, FORTY**


**FOUR MARCHES.** *See* **MARCHES, FOUR**

**52    FRUSTRATION WALTZ (1956)**
For piano

> *Duration:*
>> 8 minutes
>
> *First performance:*
>> 1957; Jefferson City, Missouri; Lincoln University
>
> *Note:*
>> "A descriptive piece about trying to keep cool in the heat of summer"

**53    FUGUE (1967)**
For piano

> *Duration:*
>> 4 minutes 32 seconds

**54    FULL MOON (1951)**
For cello and piano

> *Duration:*
>> 8 minutes

**55    GREENWOOD RHYTHM (1953)**
For chorus, (unison or SATB), wind ensemble: clarinets, saxophones, French horns, and trumpets, percussion, and dancers

> *Text:*
>> By John E. Price
>
> *Duration:*
>> 16 minutes 35 seconds
>
> *First performance:*
>> 1953; Booker T. Washington Chorus; Tulsa, Oklahoma
>
> *Note:*
>> "A scene about the Black main street in Tulsa", Oklahoma

**56    HARAMBEE (1968-1975)**
For orchestra

> *Duration:*
>> 11 minutes 47 seconds
>
> *Note:*
>> Title is Swahili and means "Let's All Pull Together"

**57    HETH SOLD EIN MEISKEN (1972)**
For chorus (SATB)

> *Text:*
>> By John E. Price
>
> *Dedication:*
>> To James and Rosamond Johnson Ensemble of Florida Memorial
>> College, Miami
>
> *Duration:*
>> 5 minutes
>
> *Note:*
>> Transcribed from an instrumental work by Josquin des Prés,
>> according to composer

**58    HYMN AND DEVIATION (1956)**
For brass quartet: French horn, trumpet, trombone, and tuba

> *Duration:*
>> 11 minutes 32 seconds
>
> *Two movements:*
>> Hymn; Deviation
>
> *First performance:*
>> 1957; Jefferson City, Missouri; Lincoln University
>
> *Note:*
>> Also titled *For Brass Quartet*

**59    HYMN AND SPIRITUAL (1972-1974)**
For chorus (SATB), unaccompanied

> *Text:*
>> By John E. Price
>
> *Duration:*
>> Hymn in 2 parts: 6 minutes; 5 minutes
>> Spiritual in 2 parts: 32 seconds; 55 seconds
>
> *Note:*
>> Hymn transcribed from *Hymn and Deviation*

**60    HYMNS, FORTY (1963-1972)**
For chorus (SATB) and organ or piano

> *Texts:*
>> By John E. Price

**61**  **HYMNS FOR PIANO (1954)**

> *Contents:*
> 15 pieces

**62**  **IDENTITY (1957)**
For voice and piano

> *Text:*
> By Thomas B. Aldrich
> *Dedication:*
> To Felicia Weathers
> *Duration:*
> 2 minutes 18 seconds
> *First performance:*
> 1957; Jefferson City, Missouri; Lincoln University

**63**  **IMPULSE AND DEVIATION, NOS. 1-24 (1958; 1971-1974; 1976)**
For violoncello

> *Dedication:*
> To Donald White (no. 1 (1958) )
> *No. 1 published in:*
> Floyd, Sam. *An Anthology of Music by Black Contemporary Composers*, Carbondale, Illinois; Southern Illinois University
> *Each piece is two movements*
> *First performance:*
> 1971; Charleston, Illinois; Eastern Illinois University; Donald Tracy, cello
> *Recording:*
> Tape in IU Library (IU performance)

**64**  **THE INNOCENTS (1958)**
Incidental music for piano

> *Play:*
> By William Inge from Henry James' "The Turn of the Screw"
> *First performance:*
> 1958; Cleveland, Ohio; Karamu House
> *Recording:*
> Tape available from composer
> *Note:*
> Involves plucked strings and other inner piano devices

**65**  INTRODUCTION: FIVE PIECES AND ENDING (1972-1973)
For chorus (SATB), oboe, cello, double bass, and percussion

> *Dedication:*
>> To Jan Hermansen
> *Duration:*
>> 15 minutes 43 seconds

**66**  INVENTION, NO. 1 (1952)
For piano

> *Printed in:*
>> *The Lamp*, Miami, Florida; Florida Memorial College, 1970
> *Duration:*
>> 1 minute 45 seconds
> *First performance:*
>> 1973; Miami, Florida; First Unitarian Church; Annette Cheskey, piano

**67**  INVENTION, NO. 2 (1956)
For piano

> *Duration:*
>> 1 minute 26 seconds

JESUS PIECES, TWO. *See* TRIGON

**68**  JOHN BEE SAIL (1970)
For chorus (SATB), piano, and percussion

> *Text:*
>> Bahamian folk text
> *Dedication:*
>> To James and Rosamond Johnson Ensemble of Florida Memorial College, Miami
> *Duration:*
>> 5 minutes 42 seconds
> *Note:*
>> Arrangement for a Bahamian folk song

**69**  **JOSEPH PRELUDE (1951)**
Incidental music for piano

> *Play:*
>> By Rolly Meinholtz
> *Dedication:*
>> To Rolly Meinholtz
> *Duration:*
>> 5 minutes
> *Note:*
>> About Joseph in Egypt

**70**  **THE JOURNEY OF THE MAGI (1966; revised 1968)**
Incidental music for chorus, clarinet, percussion, dancers, and narrators

> *Text:*
>> By Thomas Stearns Eliot "Journey of the Magi"
> *Duration:*
>> 15 minutes 20 seconds
> *First performance:*
>> Date ?; Miami, Florida; Florida Memorial College

**71**  **KNGOMA (1974-1975)**
For various vocal combinations, unaccompanied

> *Text:*
>> From the Mende language
> *Duration:*
>> Seven versions of various timings
> *Note:*
>> Title means: "Thank God for life"

**72**  **LAMENT (1967)**
For clarinet, trumpet, trombone, percussion, and dancers

> *Commissioned by and dedicated to:*
>> Katura Drayton
> *Duration:*
>> 13 minutes
> *First performance:*
>> 1967; Miami, Florida; Florida Memorial College

**73  LEST THOU BLESS ME (1972-1973)**
For chorus (SATB), woodwinds, brass, percussion, organ, and speakers

> *Text:*
>> By Robert Chute, his third poem on Black history
> *Duration:*
>> 16 minutes 37 seconds
> *Note:*
>> Concerns the life of Frederick Douglass

**74  A LIGHT FROM ST. AGNES (1968-1970)**
Opera for women's chorus (back stage), soprano, tenor, baritone solos, small orchestra, and Dixieland ensemble

> *Dedication:*
>> To Ann Flagg
> *Duration:*
>> 1 hour
> *Note:*
>> Tragedy set in the back woods of Louisiana

**75  LINE I (1967)**
For bassoon

> *Duration:*
>> 1 minute 50 seconds
> *First performance:*
>> 1968; St. Louis, Missouri, Washington University

**76  A LITANY AT ATLANTA (1978)**
For chorus (SATB) and speakers, unaccompanied

> *Text:*
>> By W. E. B. DuBois
> *Duration:*
>> 15 minutes 28 seconds

**77  A LITURGY FOR SEVEN MEMORIES (1973)**
For chorus (SATB), mezzo-soprano and baritone solos, speakers, 2 flutes, 2 oboes, 2 clarinets, organ/piano, percussion, and string septet

> *Text:*
>> By John Tagliabue

*Duration:*
>1 hour 10 minutes

*First performance:*
>1973; Miami, Florida; Florida Memorial College

*Notes:*
>Written for the James and Rosamond Johnson Ensemble of Florida Memorial College.
>
>"A liturgy expounding the world's problems and thoughts about the Christ Child within the 20th century."

**78 THE MAGIC APPLE (1958)**
Incidental music for voice and piano and dancers

>*Children's play:*
>>By Ann Flagg
>
>*Dedication:*
>>To Ann Flagg
>
>*Three acts*
>*First performance:*
>>1958; Cleveland, Ohio; Karamu House

**79 MAGNIFICAT (1974; revised 1978)**
For chorus (SATB), alto and baritone solos, organ, woodwinds, and brass

>*Text:*
>>By W. E. B. DuBois
>
>*Duration:*
>>35 minutes 20 seconds

**80 MARCH (1954)**
For band

>*Duration:*
>>4 minutes 6 seconds

**81 MARCH, NO. 1 IN C MINOR (1951)**
For band with piano

>*Dedication:*
>>To Booker T. Washington Band
>
>*Duration:*
>>17 minutes

**82**  MARCH, NO. 2 (1953)
For band with piano

>  *Duration:*
>> 16 minutes 40 seconds

**83**  MARCHES, FOUR (1969-1971)
For band

>  *Note:*
>> Concert pieces

**84**  MEDITATION AND CHANGE OF THOUGHT (1954)
For brass ensemble: French horn, trumpet, trombone, and tuba

>  *Duration:*
>> 9 minutes
>  *First performance:*
>> May 2, 1976; Charleston, Illinois; Eastern Illinois University,
>> Eastern Illinois Symphony

**85**  MEDITATION FOR APRIL THIRD (1956)
For organ

>  *Duration:*
>> 4 minutes 17 seconds
>  *First performance:*
>> April 3, 1956; Tulsa, Oklahoma; Vernon AME Church, Cleo Ross
>> Meeken, organ
>  *Note:*
>> Written for the funeral of composer's mother

**86**  MINIATURE WALTZES (1950)
For piano

>  *Contents:*
>> Twelve waltzes

**87**  MISTS (1962)
For chorus (SATB), unaccompanied

>  *Text:*
>> By Henry David Thoreau
>  *Duration:*
>> 4 minutes

**88  MORNING AIR IN SPRING (1958)**
For voice and piano

> *Text:*
>> By John E. Price
> *Duration:*
>> 2 minutes 15 seconds


**89  MUSIC FOR "12" PUPPET PLAYS (1966-1972)**
Incidental music for various combinations of instruments

> *Text:*
>> By John Tagliabue
> *Note:*
>> Written for television


**90  MUSIC FOR WOYENGI (1972)**
Incidental music for chorus, soloists, instruments, and dancers

> *Play:*
>> By Obotunde Ijemere, based on a Yoruba tale
> *One act*
> *First performance:*
>> March 16-17, 1972; Miami, Florida; Florida Memorial College


**91  MY SWEET LORD (1971)**
For piano

> *Commissioned:*
>> By Charles Hansen Publications
> *Duration:*
>> 3 minutes 40 seconds
> *Note:*
>> Instrumental arrangement of a spiritual


**NINE PIECES FOR MARCARBAR.** *See* **PIECES FOR MARCARBAR, NINE**


**92  NOAH (1963)**
Incidental music for voice and piano

> *Text:*
>> By E. Y. Harburgh

*Duration:*
>   4 minutes 20 seconds

*First performance:*
>   1963; Germany; AMS Players of Atlanta, Georgia

*Note:*
>   To be included in the musical "Jamaica"

**93   NOCTURNE FOR A WINTER NIGHT (1956)**
For French horn, harp, and strings

> *Dedication:*
>>   To Burton Hardin
>
> *Duration:*
>>   7 minutes 48 seconds
>
> *Note:*
>>   Inspired by a poem by John E. Price

**94   OCTOBER PIECES, TWO (1976)**
For clarinet and piano

> *Duration:*
>>   12 minutes

**95   OLMEC HYMN (1978)**
For voices and percussion

> *Duration:*
>>   14 minutes 22 seconds

**96   OPENING PRAYER (1978)**
For gospel choir and soloist

> *Text:*
>>   By John E. Price
>
> *Commissioned by and dedicated to:*
>>   Unity Gospel Choir, Eastern Illinois University
>
> *Duration:*
>>   6 minutes
>
> *First performance:*
>>   December 2, 1978; Charleston, Illinois; Eastern Illinois University,
>>   Unity Gospel Choir

**97  THE OTHER FOOT (1972-1974)**
Opera for large chorus (SATB), soprano and baritone soloists, 2 or 3 children's
voices, orchestra, band, and marimba

> *Text:*
>> By Ray Bradbury
>
> *Commissioned:*
>> By Napoleon Reed of The Community of Artists
>
> *Duration:*
>> 1 hour 16 minutes
>
> *One act*

**98  OVERTURE (1972-1973)**
For orchestra

> *Duration:*
>> 7 minutes 42 seconds

**99  PATER NOSTER (1972)**
For chorus (SATB) and organ

> *Text:*
>> The Lord's Prayer
>
> *Duration:*
>> 9 minutes

**100  THE PATIENCE THAT OUTLASTS CHAINS (1969)**
For 3 speakers, chorus (SATB), percussion, and harp

> *Text:*
>> By Robert Chute
>
> *Unpublished score* (IU)
>
> *Duration:*
>> 30 minutes
>
> *First performance:*
>> 1971; Miami, Florida; Florida Memorial College

**101  PIANO PIECES FOR NATACHIA AND KITTY (1975)**

> *Commissioned by and dedicated to:*
>> Sarah Wood
>
> *First performance:*
>> 1977; Bronxville, New York; Concordia College; selected pieces
>> performed at First Festival of Black Piano Music
>
> *Note:*
>> 14 intermediate pieces for young piano students

**02  PIANO SONATA NO.1 (1954; revised 1957)**

> *Dedication:*
> To Gwendolyn Belcher
> *Duration:*
> 20 minutes
> *Contents:*
> 1. Prairie
> 2. Folk Song
> 3. Square Dance
> *First performance:*
> 1957; Jefferson City, Missouri; Lincoln University

**03  PIANO SONATA NO. 2 (1958)**

> *Commissioned:*
> By A. L. Kimbrough
> *Duration:*
> 19 minutes 30 seconds
> *Three movements*
> *First performance:*
> 1970; Charleston, Illinois; Eastern Illinois University
> *Recording:*
> Tape in IU Library (IU performance)

**04  PIECE AND DEVIATION (1962)**
For viola and piano

> *Dedication:*
> To Shirley M. Wall
> *Duration:*
> 9 minutes
> *First performance:*
> 1962; Tulsa, Oklahoma, Vernon AME Church

**05  PIECE 1 (1969)**
For organ

> *Duration:*
> 5 minutes 15 seconds

**106**  **PIECES, FIVE (1972)**
For tuba

> *Dedication:*
>> To Wellington Gilbert
>
> *Duration:*
>> 8 minutes 15 seconds

**107**  **PIECES, THREE (1970)**
For string orchestra

> *Dedication:*
>> To Eastern Illinois University String Orchestra, Donald Tracy, conductor
>
> *Duration:*
>> 25 minutes
>
> *Contents:*
>> 1. Blues
>> 2. Juba
>> 3. Dance

**108**  **PIECES, TWO (1955-1975)**
For strings and brass quartet

> *Duration:*
>> 12 minutes 32 seconds
>
> *Contents:*
>> 1. The Solent
>> 2. Inertia

**109**  **PIECES, TWO (1974-1975)**
For trumpet and strings

> *Duration:*
>> 13 minutes 32 seconds
>
> *Contents:*
>> 1. Spiritual
>> 2. Jumpin' Dance

**110**  **PIECES FOR HARPSICHORD (1972-1973)**

> *Dedication:*
>> To Ruthie Tiegal
>
> *Twelve pieces*
>
> *First performance:*
>> 1976; Charleston, Illinois; Eastern Illinois University

**111 PIECES FOR MARCARBAR, NINE (1976-1978)**
For violin and piano

> *Commissioned:*
> > By Barbara Schlauch
> *Dedication:*
> > To the Schlauch family
> *Note:*
> > Six additional pieces (1977-1978)

**112 PIECES FOR MY FRIEND GATO (1974)**
For piano

> *Dedication:*
> > To Mary Ann Bialek and friend Gato
> *"9 pieces on the activities of a smart cat"*

**113 POPULAR SONGS (1950)**
For voice and piano

> *Four songs, no titles*

**114 PRAYER (1972)**
For chorus (SSAATTBB) with baritone solo, unaccompanied

> *Text:*
> > By John Tagliabue
> *Dedication:*
> > To Martin Luther King
> *Published in:*
> > Floyd, Sam. *An Anthology of Music by Black Contemporary Composers*, Carbondale, Illinois, Southern Illinois University
> *Duration:*
> > 12 minutes 10 seconds

**115 PRELUDE AND FUGUE IN C MINOR (1956)**
For piano

> *Dedication:*
> > To O. A. Fuller
> *Duration:*
> > 13 minutes

**116**    **PSALM 23 (1974)**
For chorus (SATB), unaccompanied

> *Dedication:*
>> To First Presbyterian Church Choir of Charleston, Illinois,
>> Barbara Sullivan, conductor
>
> *Duration:*
>> 9 minutes 16 seconds

**117**    **PSALM 117 (1968)**
For chorus (SATB), unaccompanied

> *Duration:*
>> 3 minutes

**118**    **PSALM 133 (1974)**
For chorus (SATB) with organ

> *Dedication:*
>> To First Presbyterian Church Choir of Charleston, Illinois,
>> Barbara Sullivan, conductor
>
> *Duration:*
>> 5 minutes 12 seconds

**119**    **PSALM 134 (1974)**
For unison chorus with organ

> *Dedication:*
>> To First Presbyterian Church Choir of Charleston, Illinois,
>> Barbara Sullivan, conductor
>
> *Duration:*
>> 6 minutes

**120**    **PSALM 2000 (1957)**
For chorus (SATB), baritone solo, with woodwinds, brass, and percussion

> *Text:*
>> By John E. Price
>
> *Duration:*
>> 16 minutes 40 seconds

**21    A PTAH HYMN (1978)**
For unaccompanied cello

> *Commissioned by and dedicated to:*
>> Gretchen Tracy
> *Duration:*
>> 12 minutes
> *First performance:*
>> April 23, 1979; Charleston, Illinois; Eastern Illinois University;
>> Gretchen Tracy, cello


**22    QUARTET (1962)**
For bassoon, French horn, violin, and viola

> *Dedication:*
>> To Bela Rozsa
> *Duration:*
>> 13 minutes 30 seconds
> *First performance:*
>> November 14, 1967; New Brunswick, New Jersey; Rutgers
>> University; Rutgers University Contemporary Chamber Ensemble
> *Recording:*
>> Tape available from composer


**123    RAG IN F MAJOR (1964)**
For piano

> *Duration:*
>> 4 minutes 10 seconds


**24    RAG IN F ♯ MAJOR (1957)**
For piano

> *Duration:*
>> 3 minutes 26 seconds


**25    RAG MASS I (1972-1974)**
For chorus (SATB), soprano, tenor, and bass solos, and rag ensemble

> *Duration:*
>> 35 minutes
> *Note:*
>> Uses rag and blues styles

**126**  **RAGS FOR PEOPLE AND FRIENDS (1976)**
For piano

> *15 pieces*

**127**  **RAIN (1952; revised 1956)**
For chorus (SATB) and piano

> *Text:*
>> By John E. Price
>
> *Dedication:*
>> To Booker T. Washington Chorus of Tulsa, Oklahoma
>
> *Duration:*
>> 5 minutes 45 seconds

**128**  **RETURN HOME (1959)**
Ballet for piano

> *Commissioned:*
>> By Hank Nystrom
>
> *Dedication:*
>> To Karamu Dance Theater
>
> *Duration:*
>> 20 minutes 53 seconds
>
> *First performance:*
>> 1959; Cleveland, Ohio; Karamu House
>
> *Note:*
>> First scene and dance withdrawn and restructured for revision of
>> *The Ballad of Candy Man Beechum*

**129**  **RHAPSODY SYMPHONIQUE (1950)**
For piano and orchestra

> *Duration:*
>> 14 minutes 30 seconds
>
> *Note:*
>> Revised as *Scherzo II*

**130**  **RIGHT ON, BABY! (1971-1972)**
Opera for soprano, tenor, baritone, and small orchestra

> *Text:*
>> By Lewis Allan

*Duration:*
40 minutes 42 seconds
*Note:*
Comedy about a very busy expectant mother


**131**   **RISIBLE VISIBLE (1957)**
Incidental music for voice, piano, and electronic sounds

*Text:*
By Elizabeth Downing
*First performance:*
1958; Cleveland, Ohio, Karamu House


**132**   **ROMANCE NO.1 (1952)**
For piano

*Dedication:*
To Margaret Porter
*Duration:*
7 minutes
*First performance:*
1957; Jefferson City, Missouri; Lincoln University


**133**   **ROMANCE NO. 2 (1953)**
For piano

*Dedication:*
To Margaret Porter
*Duration:*
5 minutes 30 seconds
*First performance:*
1957; Jefferson City, Missouri; Lincoln University


**134**   **ROMANCE NO. 3 (1953)**
For piano

*Dedication:*
To Margaret Porter
*Duration:*
3 minutes

**135** **ROMANCE NO. 4 (1955)**
For piano

> *Dedication:*
>> To Margaret Porter
> *Duration:*
>> 3 minutes 12 seconds

**136** **ROMANCE NO. 5 (1955)**
For piano

> *Dedication:*
>> To Margaret Porter
> *Duration:*
>> 4 minutes 50 seconds

**137** **"ROUNDS" FOR THE 12th OF THE MONTH (1974)**
For unaccompanied voices (soprano, alto, tenor, bass)

> *Text:*
>> By John E. Price
> *Seven rounds*

**138** **SAINT MOSES (1973-1974)**
For men's chorus with altos, soloists, narrator, woodwinds, percussion, and organ

> *Text:*
>> By John E. Price
> *Dedication:*
>> To Reverend Ben H. Hill
> *Duration:*
>> 21 minutes

**139** **ST. PETER RELATES AN INCIDENT (1973)**
For chorus (SATB), soprano, tenor, and bass soloists, readers, small band, and organ

> *Text:*
>> By James Weldon Johnson
> *Dedication:*
>> To the James and Rosamond Johnson Ensemble of Florida
>>> Memorial College, Miami
> *Duration:*
>> 15 minutes 17 seconds

**140**   SCHERZO FOR 'CELLO AND ORCHESTRA (1973)

> *Dedication:*
> To Donald Tracy
> *Duration:*
> 11 minutes 32 seconds

**141**   SCHERZO I FOR CLARINET AND ORCHESTRA (PIANO) (1952; revised 1953-1954)

> *Dedication:*
> To James Tilman
> *Duration:*
> 15 minutes
> *First performances:*
> (Piano reduction): 1954; Jefferson City, Missouri; Lincoln University.
> November 5, 1971; Miami, Florida; Radio Station WTMI; Alex Foster, clarinet; Oakland Youth Symphony; Robert Hughes, conductor.
> *Recordings:*
> Tape available from composer (with orchestra)
> Tape in IU Library (IU performance) (with piano)
> *Note:*
> Orchestrated in 1956

**142**   SCHERZO II FOR CLARINET AND ORCHESTRA (1957)

> *Duration:*
> 15 minutes 25 seconds
> *Note:*
> Revision of *Rhapsody Symphonique*

**143**   SCHERZO III FOR CLARINET AND ORCHESTRA (1969)

> *Duration:*
> 17 minutes
> *Note:*
> Uses smaller orchestra than that required for Scherzi I and II

**144**   SCHERZO IV FOR CLARINET AND ORCHESTRA (1968)

> *Duration:*
> 14 minutes 27 seconds

**145**   **SEA CALM (1978)**
For voice (high) and piano

> *Text:*
>> By Langston Hughes
>
> *Duration:*
>> 7 minutes
>
> *First performance:*
>> April 23, 1979; Charleston, Illinois; Eastern Illinois University;
>> Barbara Sullivan, soprano

**SECOND SET OF PIECES FOR CHILDREN.** *See* **SET OF PIECES FOR CHILDREN, SECOND**

**146**   **SERENADE FOR DUSK (1952)**
For voice and piano

> *Text:*
>> By John E. Price
>
> *Dedication:*
>> To Rolly Meinholtz
>
> *Duration:*
>> 13 minutes
>
> *First performance:*
>> September 26, 1975; Detroit, Michigan; William Warfield

**147**   **SERENADE FOR TULSA (1950)**
For piano and orchestra

> *Dedication:*
>> To the Tulsa (Oklahoma) Philharmonic
>
> *Duration:*
>> 13 minutes 21 seconds

**148**   **SERMON (1956)**
For chorus (SATB), unaccompanied

> *Text:*
>> By John E. Price
>
> *Dedication:*
>> To the 100th anniversary of Lincoln University, Jefferson City,
>> Missouri, and its concert choir
>
> *Duration:*
>> 6 minutes

**149** **SET NO. 1 (1959)**
For voice and piano

> *Text:*
>> By John Donne and Solomon
> *Duration:*
>> 14 minutes 31 seconds
> *Contents:*
>> 3 parts: Hymn; Ode 13; Amen
> *First performance:*
>> 1962; Tulsa, Oklahoma

**150** **A SET OF LITTLE PIECES ON KNGOMA (1974)**
For piano

> *Dedication:*
>> To "Arnold"
> *11 pieces*

**151** **SET OF PIECES FOR CHILDREN, SECOND (1976)**
For piano

> *23 pieces*

**152** **SETS OF PIECES, FIVE (1972-1974)**
For 2 and 3-part children's chorus and piano

> *Text:*
>> By John E. Price
> *Commissioned:*
>> By Floyd Johnson for his junior high school choir
> *Each set contains two pieces*

**SEVEN CAROLS FOR CHILDREN'S CHOIR AND PIANO.** *See* **CAROLS FOR CHILDREN'S CHOIR AND PIANO, SEVEN**

**153** **. . . SIMON, YES, BLACK SIMON! (1976)**
For chorus (SATB), unaccompanied

> *Text:*
>> Biblical
> *Duration:*
>> 9 minutes 20 seconds
> *Three settings about Simon of Cyrene*

**154    A SKETCH (1957)**
For chorus (SATB) and four flutes

>    *Text:*
>        By John E. Price
>    *Duration:*
>        3 minutes


**155    SKY, LAND, SEA (1973)**
For chorus (SATB), unaccompanied

>    *Text:*
>        By Della Williams
>    *Dedication:*
>        To Coach and Mrs. S. Williams
>    *Duration:*
>        4 minutes 12 seconds


**156    SONATA (1971)**
For 2 pianos

>    *Dedication:*
>        To Karen and George Sanders
>    *Duration:*
>        18 minutes 15 seconds
>    *Three movements:*
>        Middle Passage; Blues; Chica


**SONATA FOR BASS HORN AND PIANO.** *See* **SONATA FOR TUBA AND PIANO**


**157    SONATA FOR CLARINET AND PIANO (1958)**

>    *Duration:*
>        14 minutes 22 seconds
>    *Three movements*


**158    SONATA FOR TROMBONE AND PIANO (1968)**

>    *Dedication:*
>        To David Baker

*Duration:*

14 minutes 42 seconds

*Two movements:*

March; Clausula

*First performance:*

Spring 1969; St. Louis, Missouri; Washington University (First movement, only)

**159**  **SONATA FOR TUBA AND PIANO (1956)**

*Dedication:*

To John Smith

*Duration:*

16 minutes 15 seconds

*Two movements*

*First performance:*

1957; Jefferson City, Missouri; Lincoln University

*Note:*

a.k.a. *Sonata for Bass Horn and Piano*

**160**  **SONATA II FOR TUBA AND PIANO (1974-1975**

*Commissioned:*

By John Smith

*Dedication:*

To O. A. Fuller

*Duration:*

16 minutes 17 seconds

*Contents:*

1. Recitation
2. Rag
3. Spiritual

*Note:*

Written on the retirement of O. A. Fuller as Chairman of the Music Department at Lincoln University, Jefferson City, Missouri

**161**  **SONATINA NO. 1 FOR PIANO (1956)**

*Duration:*

15 minutes

*Three movements*

162    **SONATINA NO. 2 FOR PIANO (1958)**

*Duration:*
15 minutes
*Three movements*


163    **SONATINA NO. 3 FOR PIANO (1971)**

*Duration:*
13 minutes 40 seconds
*Three movements*


164    **SONG OF THE LIBERTY BELL (1976-1978)**
For chorus (SATB), baritone, 3 speakers, and orchestra

*Text:*
By Lewis Allan
*Commissioned:*
By Lewis Allan
*Duration:*
1 hour 10 minutes


165    **SONG ON A POEM BY BLAKE (1969)**
For voice and piano

*Dedication:*
To Harold Blumenfeld
*Duration:*
7 minutes


166    **SONGS FOR SPRING (1958)**
For children's chorus and piano

*Text:*
By John E. Price
*Dedication:*
To Gwendolyn Tate
*Duration:*
7 minutes 8 seconds

**167**    **SONGS ON POEMS BY DELLA WILLIAMS, TWO (1970)**
For voice and piano

>*Duration:*
>>8 minutes 32 seconds
>
>*Contents:*
>>1. Sun, Sky and Sea
>>2. Prayer

**168**    **SONGS ON POEMS BY JOHN TAGLIABUE, THREE (1967-1968)**
For voice and piano

>*Commissioned by and dedicated to:*
>>Vivan Woods
>
>*Duration:*
>>15 minutes 15 seconds
>
>*Contents:*
>>1. Cast Out, Cast Out
>>2. The Wide Expanse of Roots
>>3. The Tears

**169**    **SPIRITUAL (1972-1974)**
For clarinet and string orchestra

>*Duration:*
>>6 minutes 13 seconds

**170**    **SPIRITUAL FOR PIANO (1958)**

>*Dedication:*
>>To "Aunt Jay"
>
>*Duration:*
>>6 minutes 7 seconds
>
>*First performance:*
>>1960; Tulsa, Oklahoma; Vernon AME Church

**171**    **SPIRITUALS (1962)**
For voice and piano

>*Texts:*
>>Spirituals
>
>*Dedication:*
>>To Cleo R. Meeker

*Duration:*
10 minutes
*Four spirituals, untitled*
*First performance:*
1962; Tulsa, Oklahoma

**172   SPIRITUALS, FIFTEEN (1969)**
For voice and piano
*Texts:*
Spirituals
*Dedication:*
To Leontyne Price
*Untitled*

**173   SPIRITUALS FOR THE YOUNG PIANIST (SET I) (1978)**

*Dedication:*
To Professor and Mrs. Horace F. Mitchell
*Publication:*
New York: Belwin-Mills, 1979
*23 arrangements of traditional and original spirituals*

**174   SPIRITUALS FOR THE YOUNG PIANIST (SET II) (1978)**

*Dedication:*
To the memory of James O'Bannon
*27 arrangements of traditional and original spirituals*

**175   SPIRITUALS FOR THE YOUNG PIANIST (SET III) (1978)**

*Dedication:*
To the memory of Lee John Oliver, Sr.
*30 arrangements of traditional and original spirituals*

**176   "STEADY WAH NO MO' " (1973)**
For string orchestra
*Duration:*
8 minutes 31 seconds
*Note:*
Paraphrase on the spiritual

**177   STEAL AWAY (1966)**
For chorus (SATB), unaccompanied

> *Text:*
>> Spiritual
>
> *Dedication:*
>> To the Florida Memorial College Concert Choir, Miami
>
> *Duration:*
>> 4 minutes
>
> *First performance:*
>> 1966; Florida Memorial College, Miami

**178   STUDY IN C MAJOR (1952)**
For piano

> *Dedication:*
>> To the H. F. Mitchells
>
> *Duration:*
>> 10 minutes
>
> *First performance:*
>> Spring 1953; Tulsa, Oklahoma; Mitchell Studio

**179   STUDY IN SIXTHS (1956)**
For piano

> *Duration:*
>> 4 minutes
>
> *First performance:*
>> 1957; Jefferson City, Missouri; Lincoln University

**180   SUGGESTION FOR THE CENTURY (1954; revised (1958)**
For men's vocal quartet with orchestra

> *Dedication:*
>> To Mr. and Mrs. Russell Jelliffe of Karamu House and President
>> and Mrs. John F. Kennedy
>
> *Duration:*
>> 5 minutes 42 seconds

**181   TARANTELLA (1952; revised 1955)**
For violin and piano

> *Dedication:*
>> To Kathryn Walker
>
> *Duration:*
>> 12 minutes 32 seconds

**182**  THE TEMPEST (1965)
Incidental music for chorus (SATB), flute, guitar, and trumpet

> *Text:*
>> By William Shakespeare
>
> *First performance:*
>> 1965; Atlanta, Georgia; AMS Players

THREE PIECES. *See* PIECES, THREE

THREE SONGS ON POEMS BY JOHN TAGLIABUE. *See* SONGS ON POEMS BY JOHN TAGLIABUE, THREE

THREE VARIANTS. *See* VARIANTS, THREE

**183**  TO THE SHRINE OF THE BLACK MADONNA (1974)
For string orchestra

> *Dedication:*
>> To Donald Tracy and the Eastern Illinois University String Ensemble
>
> *Duration:*
>> 13 minutes 55 seconds
>
> *Note:*
>> "Before Notre Dame in Paris was built, there was a 'Shrine to the Black Madonna' "

**184**  TOBIAS AND THE ANGEL (1958)
Incidental music for a play for voice, harp, and percussion

> *Commissioned:*
>> By Reuben Silver
>
> *First performance:*
>> 1959; Cleveland, Ohio; Karamu House

**185**  TRIGON (1957)
For chorus (SATB), unaccompanied

> *Text:*
>> By John E. Price
>
> *Duration:*
>> 15 minutes
>
> *Note:*
>> Revised as *Two Jesus Pieces*

**186**  **TRIO (1952)**
For oboe, English horn, and bassoon

>*Duration:*
>>10 minutes 13 seconds

**187**  **TRIO (1960; revised 1974)**
For violin, cello, and piano

>*Dedication:*
>>To Shirley Wall, Floyd Johnson, and Betty Kimble
>*Duration:*
>>16 minutes 12 seconds
>*Two movements*

**188**  **TRIO (1968)**
For clarinet, French horn, and tuba

>*Duration:*
>>13 minutes
>*First performance:*
>>(first movement only): Spring 1969; St. Louis, Missouri; Washington University

**189**  **TUTANKHAMEN: TRUMPETS (1976-1978)**
For trumpet, trumpet (tape), strings, and percussion

>*Dedication:*
>>To Louis and Kathy Ranger
>*Duration:*
>>17 minutes

**190**  **TWELFTH NIGHT (1959)**
Incidental music for unaccompanied voice

>*Text:*
>>By William Shakespeare
>*First performance:*
>>1958; Cleveland, Ohio; Karamu House

**TWO CAROLS.** *See* **CAROLS, TWO**

TWO JESUS PIECES. *See* TRIGON


TWO OCTOBER PIECES. *See* OCTOBER PIECES, TWO


TWO PIECES. *See* PIECES, TWO


TWO SONGS ON POEMS BY DELLA WILLIAMS. *See* SONGS ON POEMS BY DELLA WILLIAMS, TWO


**191**  **TWO TYPED LINES (1959; revised 1962)**
For voice and piano

> *Text:*
> > By "Shelley of Cleveland"
> *Printed in:*
> > *The Lamp*, Miami, Florida, Florida Memorial College, 1969
> *Duration:*
> > 1 minute 5 seconds
> *First performances:*
> > April 13, 1972; Lawrence, Kansas; University of Kansas; Miriam Green, soprano.
> > September 26, 1975; Detroit, Michigan; William Warfield


**192**  **VARIANTS, THREE (1973)**
For piano

> *Commissioned:*
> > By Joann Rile
> *Dedication:*
> > To Leon Bates
> *Duration:*
> > 11 minutes 36 seconds


**193**  **VERSES FROM GENESIS AND PSALMS (1961)**
For clarinet, percussion, cello, narrator, and dancers

> *Commissioned:*
> > By the youth department of Boston Avenue Methodist Church, Tulsa, Oklahoma

*Dedication:*
>To Mable Lynch

*Duration:*
>20 minutes 55 seconds

*First performance:*
>October, 1961; Tulsa, Oklahoma; Boston Avenue Methodist Church


**194**    **WE WEAR THE MASK (1973)**
For chorus (SATB), unaccompanied

>*Text:*
>>By Paul Laurence Dunbar

>*Duration:*
>>5 minutes 48 seconds


**195**    **WHAT MONTH WAS JESUS BORN? (1970)**
For chorus (SATB), mezzo-soprano solo, and piano

>*Text:*
>>Spiritual

>*Duration:*
>>6 minutes 28 seconds

>*First performance:*
>>December 1970; Miami, Florida; Florida Memorial College

*Noah Francis Ryder*

## NOAH FRANCIS RYDER
*b. Nashville, Tennessee, April 10, 1914; d. Norfolk, Virginia, April 17, 1964*


Ryder entered Hampton Institute in 1931 where, as a student, he arranged music, performed as a pianist, and conducted college choral groups. He formed a singing group known as the Deep River Boys, which later became internationally famous. At Hampton he was particularly influenced by Nathaniel Dett, Clarence Cameron White, and Ernest Hays. As a senior music student he presented an entire program of his works. In 1935 Ryder received his Bachelor of Science degree in music. The University of Michigan awarded him a Master of Music degree in 1947.

Following a position as music supervisor for a Goldsboro, North Carolina public high school, Ryder became the director of the music department at Palmer Memorial Institute in Sedalia, North Carolina in 1936. In 1938 he moved to Winston-Salem where he assumed a similar position at Teachers College. From 1941 to 1944 he was head of the theory department at Hampton Institute and director of the famed Hampton Institute Choir. In addition, he became the director of the Harry T. Burleigh Glee Club of Hampton, Virginia. Ryder served in the Navy from 1944 to 1946. Following his Master's degree in 1947, he joined the faculty at Virginia State College in Norfolk as head of the music department and choir director. He also resumed his formed position as director of the Harry T. Burleigh Glee Club. He served in these positions until 1962. In spite of all these activities, he still continued to compose and arrange, and in 1948 he received the annual Achievement Award for creative work from the Norfolk Chapter of Omega Psi Phi fraternity. Two years later he was again honored by Delta Sigma Theta sorority. In the early 1950's he founded the

*259*

Norfolk Staters, a group which grew out of musical activities at Virginia State College.

Ryder was a member of ASCAP, the American Guild of Organists, the Music Educator's National Conference, the Virginia Teachers Association, the American Federation of Musicians, and the Association of Music Teachers in Negro Colleges.

He was buried with military honors at the National Cemetery in Hampton, Virginia.

*Sources:*

Information submitted by ASCAP, Dr. Georgia Ryder,
    Marjorie S. Johnson, and Virginia State College
ASCAP 1966
Cl
I-Who 1951
Johnson, Marjorie S. *Noah Francis Ryder (1914-1964): A Study
    of His Life, Works, and Contributions to Music Education*,
    Washington, D. C., Catholic University, Master's thesis, 1968
- - - - "Noah Francis Ryder: Composer and Educator," in *The Black
    Perspective in Music*, vol. 6, no. 1 (Spring 1978), pp. 19-31
SoM
To
Wh
Who-C 1951

*Unpublished works are available from Dr. Georgia Ryder*

**1 AN' I CRY**
For chorus (SATB) with soprano solo, unaccompanied

> *Text:*
>> Spiritual
> *Dedication:*
>> To Kemper Herrald and the Spellman-Morehouse Choral Union, Atlanta, Georgia
> *Publication:*
>> New York: Handy Bros., 1939 (HU)

**2 BALM IN GILIAD (sic)**
For chorus (SATB) with tenor solo, unaccompanied

> *Text:*
>> Spiritual
> *Publication:*
>> New York: Handy Bros., 1938 (HU)

**3 BE READY WHEN HE COMES (c. 1944)**
For men's chorus (TTBB), unaccompanied

> *Text:*
>> Spiritual
> *Unpublished*

**4 BETHLEHEM LULLABY**
For chorus (SATB) with soprano solo, unaccompanied

> *Text:*
>> Traditional Negro folk song
> *Publication:*
>> Boston, Massachusetts: R. D. Row, 1946 (HU)

**5 BY AND BY**
For chorus (SATB) with soprano solo, unaccompanied

> *Text:*
>> Spiritual
> *Dedication:*
>> To Walnut Hills High School (composer's alma mater), Cincinnati, Ohio
> *Publication:*
>> New York: Handy Bros., 1938 (HU)

**6  COULDN'T HEAR NOBODY PRAY (c. 1944)**
For men's chorus (TTBB) with solo, unaccompanied

>*Text:*
>>Spiritual
>*Unpublished*


**7  CRUCIFIXION (c. 1944)**
For men's chorus (TTBB), unaccompanied

>*Text:*
>>Spiritual
>*Unpublished*


**8  DEAR NORFOLK STATE**
For chorus (SATB), unaccompanied

>*School song*
>*Unpublished*


**9  DONE PAID MY VOW**
For chorus (SATB), unaccompanied

>*Text:*
>>Spiritual
>*Dedication:*
>>To Sedalia Singers of the Palmer Memorial Institute, Sedalia,
>>North Carolina
>*Publication:*
>>New York: Handy Bros., 1938 (HU)


**10  DON'T BE A WEARY TRAVELER**
For chorus (SSAATTBB) with alto solo, unaccompanied

>*Text:*
>>Spiritual
>*Dedication:*
>>To composer's a cappella choir, Winston-Salem Teachers College,
>>North Carolina
>*Publication:*
>>New York: Handy Bros., 1939 (HU)

**11**  **EVERY TIME I FEEL THE SPIRIT (c. 1944)**
For men's chorus (TTBB) with solo, unaccompanied

> *Text:*
>> Spiritual
> *Unpublished*


**FIVE SKETCHES FOR PIANO.** *See* **SKETCHES FOR PIANO, FIVE**


**12**  **GLORY, HALLELUIA (c. 1944)**
For men's chorus (TTBB), unaccompanied

> *Text:*
>> Spiritual
> *Unpublished*


**13a**  **GONNA JOURNEY AWAY**
Anthem for men's chorus (TTBB), unaccompanied

> *Text:*
>> By Noah Ryder
> *Publication:*
>> New York: Handy Bros., 1938
> *Note:*
>> Analysis in: Johnson, Marjorie S. *Noah Francis Ryder (1914-1964): A Study of His Life, Works, and Contributions to Music Education*, Washington, D. C., Catholic University, Master's thesis, 1968, pp. 48-51


**13b**  **GONNA JOURNEY AWAY**
For chorus (SATB) with baritone and alto solos, unaccompanied

> *Publication:*
>> New York: Handy Bros., 1939 (HU)


**14**  **GREAT DAY**
For chorus (SATB), unaccompanied

> *Text:*
>> Spiritual
> *Publication:*
>> New York: Handy Bros., 1938 (HU)

**15    GWINE UP**

For chorus (SATB) with baritone solo, unaccompanied

> *Text:*
>> Spiritual
>
> *Dedication:*
>> "to my Dad"
>
> *Publication:*
>> New York: Handy Bros., 1936 (HU)


**16    HALLELUIA, BEEN DOWN INTO THE SEA (c. 1944)**

For men's chorus (TTBB) with solo, unaccompanied

> *Text:*
>> Spiritual
>
> *Unpublished*


**17    HE AIN'T COMING HERE TO DIE NO MORE**

For chorus (SATB) with alto solo, unaccompanied

> *Text:*
>> Spiritual
>
> *Dedication:*
>> To Reverend D. DeWitt Wasson, Minister of Music, Epworth
>> Methodist Church, Norfolk, Virginia
>
> *Publication:*
>> Glen Rock, New Jersey: J. Fischer, 1949 (HU; LC)


**18    HEAR THE LAMBS A-CRYING**

For chorus (SATB), unaccompanied

> *Text:*
>> Spiritual
>
> *Dedication:*
>> To Virginia State University Chorus, Harold Montague, director
>
> *Publication:*
>> New York: Handy Bros., 1938 (HU)


**19    HE'S A LONG JOHN (c. 1944)**

a. For chorus (SATB), unaccompanied
b. For men's chorus (TTBB), unaccompanied

> *Text:*
>> Negro prison song
>
> *Unpublished*

**20**   HOSANNA (c. 1944)
For chorus (SATB), unaccompanied

>*Text:*
>>Spiritual
>
>*Unpublished*

**21**   I GOT A MOTHER IN HEAVEN
For chorus (SATB), unaccompanied

>*Text:*
>>Spiritual
>
>*Dedication:*
>>To Warner Lawson and his choir of Agricultural & Technical College of North Carolina at Greensboro
>
>*Publication:*
>>New York: Handy Bros., 1938 (HU)

**22**   I HEARD THE PREACHING OF THE ELDERS
Anthem for chorus (SATB) with soprano solo, unaccompanied

>*Text:*
>>Spiritual
>
>*Dedication:*
>>To Hampton Institute Choir, Gerald Burks Wilson, director
>
>*Publication:*
>>New York: Handy Bros., 1938 (HU)
>
>*Note:*
>>Analysis in: Johnson, Marjorie S. *Noah Francis Ryder (1914-1964): A Study of His Life, Works, and Contributions to Music Education*, Washington, D.C., Catholic University, Master's thesis, 1968, pp. 63-68

**23**   I WILL NEVER BETRAY MY LORD
For chorus (SATB), unaccompanied

>*Text:*
>>Spiritual
>
>*Publication:*
>>New York: Handy Bros., 1935 (HU)

**24  IN BEAUTIFUL OHIO (c. 1952)**
For voice and piano

>*Text:*
>>By Georgia Ryder
>
>*Unpublished*
>*Note:*
>>Won an award in a contest to compose a song for the state of Ohio, 1952

**25  IN BRIGHT MANSIONS ABOVE**
For chorus (SATB), unaccompanied

>*Text:*
>>Spiritual
>
>*Publication:*
>>New York: Handy Bros., 1939 (HU)
>
>*Note:*
>>Anthem

**26  JOSHUA FOUGHT THE BATTLE OF JERICHO**
For men's chorus (TTBB), unaccompanied

>*Text:*
>>Spiritual
>
>*Publication:*
>>Boston, Massachusetts: R. D. Row, 1946 (HU; LC)

**27a  LET US BREAK BREAD TOGETHER**
For chorus (SATB), unaccompanied

>*Text:*
>>Spiritual
>
>*Dedication:*
>>To Henry Booker and his glee club of Lincoln University, Lincoln, Pennsylvania
>
>*Publication:*
>>Glen Rock, New Jersey: J. Fischer, 1945 (HU; LC)
>
>*Note:*
>>Analysis in: Johnson, Marjorie S. *Noah Francis Ryder (1914-1964): A Study of His Life, Works, and Contributions to Music Education*, Washington, D. C., Catholic University, Master's thesis, 1968, pp. 61-63

**27b  LET US BREAK BREAD TOGETHER**
For chorus (SAB), unaccompanied

> *Publication*
>> Glen Rock, New Jersey: J. Fischer, 1955 (LC)

**27c  LET US BREAK BREAD TOGETHER**
For women's chorus (SSA), unaccompanied

> *Publication:*
>> Glen Rock, New Jersey: J. Fischer, 1958

**27d  LET US BREAK BREAD TOGETHER**
For men's chorus (TTBB), unaccompanied

> *Publication:*
>> Glen Rock, New Jersey: J. Fischer, 1950 (LC)

**27e  LET US BREAK BREAD TOGETHER**
For voice and piano

> *Publication:*
>> Glen Rock, New Jersey: J. Fischer, 1950 (LC); 1968 (High voice)

**28a  LITTLE DAVID PLAY ON YOUR HARP**
For women's chorus (SSAA), unaccompanied

> *Text:*
>> Spiritual
> *Publication:*
>> Boston, Massachusetts: R. D. Row, 1947 (LC)

**28b  LITTLE DAVID PLAY ON YOUR HARP**
For men's chorus (TTBB) and piano

> *Publication:*
>> Boston, Massachusetts: R. D. Row, 1947 (LC)

**29  LORD, I DON'T FEEL NO WAYS TIRED (c. 1944)**
For chorus (SATB), unaccompanied

> *Text:*
>> Spiritual
> *Unpublished*

**30  LORD, I WANT TO BE A CHRISTIAN**
For chorus (SATB), unaccompanied

>   *Text:*
>>   Spiritual
>   *Dedication:*
>>   To George Van Hoy Collins and his Dillard High School Chorus, Goldsboro, North Carolina
>   *Publication:*
>>   New York: Handy Bros., 1938 (HU)

**31  LOVE SONG**
For men's chorus (TTBB), unaccompanied

>   *Text:*
>>   By Noah Ryder
>   *Publication:*
>>   Boston, Massachusetts: R. D. Row, 1946 (HU; LC)
>   *Note:*
>>   Analysis in: Johnson, Marjorie S. *Noah Francis Ryder (1914-1964): A Study of His Life, Works, and Contributions to Music Education*, Washington, D. C., Catholic University, Master's thesis, 1968, pp. 46-47

**32  MARY BORNED A BABY**
For chorus (SATB), unaccompanied

>   *Text:*
>>   Spiritual
>   *Publication:*
>>   Boston, Massachusetts: R. D. Row, 1946 (HU; LC)

**33  MASSA DEAR (c. 1944)**
For men's chorus (TTBB), unaccompanied

>   *Text:*
>>   By Frederick Manley; traditional melody
>   *Unpublished*
>   *Note:*
>>   Ryder's comments: Possibly inspired Largo of Antonin Dvorak's *New World Symphony*

**34   MEADOWLANDS (c. 1944)**
For men's chorus (TTBBB), unaccompanied

> *Russian Cavalry song*
> *Unpublished*

**35   A MIGHTY FORTRESS IS OUR GOD**
For men's chorus (TTBB), unaccompanied

> *Text and tune:*
> By Martin Luther
> *Publication:*
> Boston, Massachusetts: R. D. Row, 1947 (HU)
> *Notes:*
> Set in anthem form.
> Analysis in: Johnson, Marjorie S. *Noah Francis Ryder (1914-1964): A Study of His Life, Works, and Contributions to Music Education*, Washington, D. C., Catholic University, Master's thesis, 1968, pp. 51-54.

**36   MY LORD IS SO HIGH**
For chorus (SATB) with soprano and tenor solos, unaccompanied

> *Text:*
> Spiritual
> *Dedication:*
> To the choir of Alabama A&M College, Normal Alabama, Samuel W. Hill, director
> *Publication:*
> New York: Handy Bros., 1939 (HU)

**37   MY LORD'S RISEN FROM THE DEAD (c. 1944)**
For chorus (SATB), unaccompanied

> *Text:*
> Spiritual
> *Unpublished*

**38   MY SOUL COULDN'T BE CONTENTED (c. 1944)**
For men's chorus (TTBB) with solo, unaccompanied

> *Text:*
> Spiritual
> *Unpublished*

**39  MY SOUL DOTH MAGNIFY THE LORD**
Anthem for chorus (SATB) with soprano solo and organ

> *Text:*
>> Bible, New Testament, Gospel according to St. Luke
> *Publication:*
>> Glen Rock, New Jersey: J. Fischer, 1958 (HU)
> *Note:*
>> Analysis in: Johnson, Marjorie S. *Noah Francis Ryder (1914-1964): A Study of His Life, Works, and Contributions to Music Education*, Washington, D. C., Catholic University Master's thesis, 1968, pp. 41-44

**40  NO MORE AUCTION BLOCK**
For chorus (SATB) with soprano solo, unaccompanied

> *Text:*
>> Spiritual
> *Dedication:*
>> To Charles Flax and his choirs of Hampton and Newport News, Virginia
> *Publication:*
>> New York: Handy Bros., 1939 (HU)
> *Note:*
>> Analysis in: Johnson, Marjorie S. *Noah Francis Ryder (1914-1964): A Study of His Life, Works, and Contributions to Music Education*, Washington, D. C., Catholic University, Master's thesis, 1968, pp. 55-56

**41  NOBODY KNOWS DE TROUBLE I SEE**
For chorus (SATB), unaccompanied

> *Text:*
>> Spiritual
> *Dedication:*
>> To Tuskegee Institute Choir
> *Publication:*
>> New York: Handy Bros., 1938 (HU; LC)

**42  NOCTURNE IN C MAJOR**
For voice and piano

> *Text:*
>> By Noah Ryder

*Publication:*
>Boston, Massachusetts: R. D. Row, 1946

*Note:*
>Analysis in: Johnson, Marjorie S. *Noah Francis Ryder (1914-1964): A Study of His Life, Works, and Contributions to Music Education*, Washington, D. C., Catholic University, Master's thesis, 1968, pp. 45-46

**43  O LEM' ME SHINE**
For chorus (SATB) with baritone solo, unaccompanied

*Text:*
>Spiritual

*Dedication:*
>To Herbert A. Lyons and his chorus of Morristown College, Morristown, Tennessee

*Publication:*
>New York: Handy Bros., 1935 (HU; LC)

*Note:*
>Analysis in: Johnson, Marjorie S. *Noah Francis Ryder (1914-1964): A Study of His Life, Works, and Contributions to Music Education*, Washington, D. C., Catholic University, Master's thesis, 1968, pp. 56-57

**44  O MY GOOD LORD, SHOW ME THE WAY (c. 1944)**
For men's chorus (TTBB), unaccompanied

*Text:*
>Spiritual

*Unpublished*

**45  OL ARK'S A MOVERIN' (c. 1944)**
For men's chorus (TTBB) with solo, unaccompanied

*Text:*
>Spiritual

*Unpublished*

**46  OVER MY HEAD (c. 1944)**
For men's chorus, unaccompanied

*Text:*
>Spiritual

*Unpublished*

**47**   THE PALMER PRAYER (c. 1936)
For chorus (SATB), unaccompanied

>   *Unpublished*

**48**   PRAYER
For chorus (SATB) with soprano solo and piano

>   *Text:*
>>   By R. J. Brown, Jr.
>   *Publication:*
>>   Glen Rock, New Jersey: J. Fischer, 1953

**49**   THE PSALM

>   *Unpublished*

**50**   RISE UP SHEPHERD AND FOLLOW (c. 1944)
For men's chorus (TTBB), unaccompanied

>   *Text:*
>>   Spiritual
>   *Unpublished*

**51**   RUN TO JESUS
For chorus (SATB) with baritone solo, unaccompanied

>   *Text:*
>>   Spiritual
>   *Dedication:*
>>   To Robert Nathaniel Dett and his Choir of Sam Houston College,
>>   Austin, Texas
>   *Publication:*
>>   New York: Handy Bros., 1936 (HU)

**52**   SCANDALIZE MY NAME (c. 1944)
For men's chorus (TTBB) with solo, unaccompanied

>   *Text:*
>>   Spiritual
>   *Unpublished*

**53   SEA SUITE (c. 1944)**
For men's chorus, unaccompanied

> *Text:*
>> By Noah Ryder
>
> *Dedication:*
>> To Maynard Klein and his Glee Club of Tulane University, New Orleans, Louisiana
>
> *Publication:*
>> New York: Handy Bros., 1946
>
> *Contents:*
> 1. Haul Away Mateys We're Almost Home
> 2. Up anchors and Away
> 3. A Sailor's Life For Me
> 4. A Sailor to His Loved One
> 5. Prayer Aboard Ship
>
> *Notes:*
>> Composed while in a naval hospital for the Navy Choir of Hampton Institute.
>>
>> No. 1 won the grand prize in Navy War Writers' Contest, 1944.
>>
>> Analysis in: Johnson, Marjorie S. *Noah Francis Ryder (1914-1964): A Study of His Life, Works, and Contributions to Music Education*, Washington, D. C., Catholic University, Master's thesis, 1968, pp. 31-40.

**54   SEE FO' AN' TWENTY ELDERS (c. 1944)**
a. For chorus (SSAATTBB), unaccompanied
b. For men's chorus (TTBB), unaccompanied

> *Text:*
>> Spiritual
>
> *Unpublished*

**55   SEE THAT BABE IN THE LOWLY MANGER**
For men's chorus (TTBB), unaccompanied

> *Text:*
>> By Noah Ryder
>
> *Publication:*
>> New York: G. Schirmer, 1946 (HU)

**56**   **SKETCHES FOR PIANO, FIVE**

> *Publication:*
>> New York: Handy Bros., 1947 (LC)
>
> *Contents:*
>> 1. Idyl
>> 2. Serenade
>> 3. Fantasie
>> 4. Poem
>> 5. Rhapsodie
>
> *Note:*
>> Analysis in: Johnson, Marjorie S. *Noah Francis Ryder (1914-1964): A Study of His Life, Works, and Contributions to Music Education*, Washington, D. C., Catholic University, Master's thesis, 1968, pp. 20-31

**57**   **SOMEBODY GOT LOST IN THE STORM (c. 1944)**
For men's chorus (TTBB), unaccompanied

> *Text:*
>> Spiritual
>
> *Unpublished*

**58**   **STAND BY ME (c. 1944)**
For solo voice with men's chorus (TTBB) hum as accompaniment

> *Text:*
>> Spiritual
>
> *Unpublished*

**59**   **STRING QUARTET**

> *Unfinished*
> *Unpublished*

**60**   **SUNRISE**
Anthem for chorus (SATB), unaccompanied

> *Text:*
>> By Noah Ryder
>
> *Dedication:*
>> To Fisk University Choir, Nashville, Tennessee

*Publication:*
>New York: Handy Bros., 1939 (HU)

*Note:*
>Analysis in: Johnson, Marjorie S. *Noah Francis Ryder (1914-1964): A Study of His Life, Works, and Contributions to Music Education*, Washington, D. C., Catholic University, Master's thesis, 1968, pp. 44

**61   SYMPHONY**

>*Unfinished*
>*Unpublished*

**62   THEM DRY BONES**
For men's chorus (TTBB), unaccompanied

>*Text:*
>>Spiritual

>*Publication:*
>>Boston, Massachusetts: R. D. Row, 1947 (HU; LC)

**63   THIS OL' HAMMER**
For men's chorus (TTBB) with tenor solo, unaccompanied

>*Text:*
>>Traditional Negro convict song

>*Publication:*
>>New York: G. Schirmer, 1947 (LC)

>*Notes:*
>>Arranged for Creative Dance Group of Hampton Institute.
>>Analysis in: Johnson, Marjorie S. *Noah Francis Ryder (1914-1964): A Study of His Life, Works, and Contributions to Music Education*, Washington, D. C., Catholic University, Master's thesis, 1968, pp. 58-60.

**64   WATER BOY (c. 1944)**
For solo voice with men's chorus (TTBB) hum as accompaniment

>*Text:*
>>Traditional Negro work song

>*Unpublished*

**65  WHAT YOU GONNA CALL YO' PRETTY LITTLE BABY?**
For men's chorus (TTBB), unaccompanied

>*Text:*
>>Spiritual
>*Dedication:*
>>To Charles Flax and the "Men of Hampton" Glee Club,
>>Hampton Institute
>*Publication:*
>>New York: G. Schirmer, 1945 (LC)

**66  WHO'LL BE A WITNESS?**
For men's chorus (TTBB) with tenor solo, unaccompanied

>*Text:*
>>Spiritual
>*Publication:*
>>New York: G. Schirmer, 1947 (LC)

*Frederick Tillis*

*b. Galveston, Texas, January 5, 1930*

Tillis earned his Master of Arts degree (1952) and Doctor's degree (1963) in music composition at the University of Iowa.

His first academic position was at Wiley College in Marshall, Texas (where he earned his Bachelor of Arts degree) as instructor and director of instrumental music. During his military service, from 1952 to 1956, he directed an air force band. Following this, he returned to Wiley College as assistant professor where he remained until 1964. In 1963 he was promoted to associate professor status. From 1964 to 1967 he was head of the theory department at Grambling College in Louisiana. This position was followed by a professorship at Kentucky State University in Frankfort, Kentucky, where he was appointed head of the music department. In 1970 he joined the faculty at the University of Massachusetts at Amherst where he is Professor of Music Theory and Composition and Director of the Afro-American Music and Jazz Program. In 1974 he was made Associate Provost and in 1976 became Special Assistant to the Provost for the Arts. The summers of 1971 and 1972 were spent in connection with various workshops and institutes in Afro-American studies. He has published a textbook, *Jazz Theory and Improvization* (New York: Charles Hansen).

Tillis was a Danforth Associate in a 1969 program to recognize and encourage good teaching. From 1969 to 1970 he was a member of the Board of Directors of the Central Kentucky Youth Orchestra. Two times he was the recipient of a United Negro College Fund Fellowship and in 1978 received a Rockefeller Foundation Grant. Several of his works have been commissioned.

He is a member of several professional organizations, among them: American

Music Center (composer member), College Music Society, National Association of Jazz Educators, Massachusetts Music Educators Association, Music Teachers National Association, in which he was the national chairman of the theory and composition section from 1969 to 1971, and the Music Educators National Conference.

*Sources:*
Information submitted by composer
An
Cl
I-Who, 1977
Ja
SoA
SoM
Who-A

*Except where indicated, compositions are unpublished and available from*
*American Composer's Alliance*

**1 ALLELUIA (1969)**
For chorus (SATB), unaccompanied

> *Duration:*
> > 7 minutes
> *First performance:*
> > 1974; Marshall, Texas; Wiley College


**2 A BALLAD OF REMEMBRANCE FOR VOICE AND PIANO (1972)**
For medium voice

> *Text:*
> > By Robert E. Hayden
> *Unpublished, available from composer*
> *Duration:*
> > 8 1/4 minutes


**3 THE BLUE EXPRESS (1973)**
For jazz ensemble

> *Unpublished, available from composer*
> *Duration:*
> > 5 minutes
> *First performance:*
> > 1973; Amherst, Massachusetts; University of Massachusetts
> > > Jazz Workshop
> *Note:*
> > Written for Jazz Workshop at University of Massachusetts


**4 BLUE STONE DIFFERENCIA (1972)**
For jazz ensemble

> *Unpublished, available from composer*
> *Duration:*
> > 5 minutes
> *First performance:*
> > 1972; Amherst, Massachusetts; University of Massachusetts
> > > Jazz Workshop
> *Note:*
> > Written for Jazz Workshop at University of Massachusetts

**5 BRASS QUINTET (1962)**

*Publication:*
New York: General Music
*Duration:*
10 minutes
*First performance:*
1972; Iowa City, Iowa; University of Iowa
*Recording:*
Serenus 12066 (1976)

**6 CAPRICCIO FOR VIOLA AND PIANO (1960)**

*Duration:*
3 minutes 30 seconds

**7 CELEBRATION (1966)**
For concert band

*Commissioned :*
By Morehouse College, Atlanta, Georgia
*Unpublished, available from composer*
*Duration:*
5 minutes 30 seconds
*First performance:*
1966; Atlanta, Georgia; Morehouse College
*Note:*
Grand march

**8 CHORALE SETTINGS FOR ORGAN, IN BAROQUE STYLE, THREE (1962)**

*Unpublished, available from composer*
*Duration:*
4 minutes

**9 CONCERT PIECE FOR CLARINET AND PIANO (1955; revised 1960)**

*Duration:*
4 minutes 45 seconds
*First performance:*
(Original version) 1959; Dallas, Texas; North Texas State University.
(Revised version) 1970; Amherst, Massachusetts; University of
Massachusetts; Jerry Chenewoth, clarinet; Dwight Peltzer, piano

**10**　CONCERTO FOR PIANO (1977)
With jazz orchestra

> *Unpublished, available from composer*
> *Duration:*
>> 19 minutes
> *First performance:*
>> 1977; Amherst, Massachusetts; University of Massachusetts Fine
>> Arts Center
> *Note:*
>> In two parts

**11**　THE COTTON CURTAIN (1966)
For orchestra

> *Duration:*
>> 4 minutes 45 seconds
> *First performance:*
>> 1966; Grambling, Louisiana; Grambling College
> *Note:*
>> For student orchestra

**12**　DESIGNS FOR ORCHESTRA NOS. 1 AND 2 (1963)

> *Durations:*
>> No. 1—7 minutes;  No. 2—5 minutes 30 seconds
> *First performance:*
>> 1968; Atlanta, Georgia; Atlanta Symphony Orchestra
> *Notes:*
>> Ph.D. dissertation; abstract in *Dissertation Abstracts* XXIX, 6,
>> 2513.
>> Can be performed separately.

**13**　THE END OF ALL FLESH (1960)
For voice (baritone) and piano

> *Text:*
>> Bible, New Testament
> *Duration:*
>> 3 minutes 30 seconds
> *First performance:*
>> 1973; Weston, Massachusetts; Regis College

**14  FANTASY (1975)**
For jazz ensemble

> *Unpublished, available from composer*
> *Duration:*
>> 10 minutes
> *First performance:*
>> November 4, 1975; Amherst, Massachusetts; University of
>> Massachusetts Jazz Workshop
> *Notes:*
>> On a theme by Julian Adderley (*A Little Taste*)
>> Written for Jazz Workshop at University of Massachusetts

**FIVE SPIRITUALS, FOR CHORUS AND BRASS CHOIR.** *See* **SPIRITUALS, FOR CHORUS AND BRASS CHOIR, FIVE**

**15  FREEDOM (1968)**
For chorus (SATB), unaccompanied

> *Commissioned:*
>> By Kentucky State College Choir, Frankfort, Kentucky
> *Publication:*
>> New York: Southern Music Publishers, 1974 (IU)
> *Duration:*
>> 8 minutes
> *First performance:*
>> 1972; Amherst, Massachusetts; University of Massachusetts;
>> University Chorale; Richard DuBois, conductor
> *Recording:*
>> Mark Custom Records MC 1849
> *Note:*
>> Memorial to Dr. Martin Luther King, Jr.

**16  HALLELUJAH (1966)**
For men's chorus, unaccompanied

> *Duration:*
>> 5 minutes 30 seconds
> *First performance:*
>> 1967; Atlanta, Georgia; Morehouse College; Morehouse Glee Club

**17** **IN A SPIRITED MOOD (1961)**
For brass quintet and baritone horn

> *To be published by Joshua Corporation, New York*
> *Duration:*
>> 4 minutes 45 seconds
> *First performance:*
>> 1965; Grambling, Louisiana; Grambling College

**18** **KCOR VARIATIONS (1977)**
For jazz orchestra

> *Unpublished, available from composer*
> *Duration:*
>> 9 1/2 minutes
> *First performance:*
>> 1977; Amherst, Massachusetts; University of Massachusetts Fine
>> Arts Center

**19** **METAMORPHOSIS ON A "SCHEME" BY J. S. BACH (1972)**
For jazz ensemble

> *To be published by Joshua Corporation, New York*
> *Duration:*
>> 5 minutes
> *First performance:*
>> 1972; Amherst, Massachusetts; University of Massachusetts
>> Jazz Workshop
> *Note:*
>> Written for Jazz Workshop at University of Massachusetts

**20** **MOTIONS FOR TROMBONE AND PIANO (1964)**

> *Duration:*
>> 10 minutes 30 seconds
> *First performance:*
>> 1965; Bloomington, Illinois; Illinois Wesleyan University,
>> Contemporary Composers Forum; Leroy Humphrey, trombone;
>> Abraham Plum, piano
> *Note:*
>> Written for Leroy Humphrey

**21  MOVEMENTS FOR PIANO, THREE (1964)**

> *Duration:*
>> 9 minutes
>
> *First performance:*
>> 1965; Bloomington, Illinois; Illinois Wesleyan University;
>> Contemporary Composers Forum; Abraham Plum, piano

**22  MUSIC FOR ALTO FLUTE, CELLO, AND PIANO (1966)**

> *Commissioned:*
>> By Trio Pro Viva
>
> *Publication:*
>> New York: Southern Music Publishers
>
> *Duration:*
>> 5 minutes 30 seconds
>
> *First performance:*
>> 1967; Frankfort, Kentucky; Kentucky State College; Trio Pro Viva:
>> Antoinette Handy, flute; Ronald Liscomb, cello; Gladys Perry
>> Norris, piano
>
> *Recording:*
>> Eastern ERS-513 (1968)

**23  MUSIC FOR AN EXPERIMENTAL LAB, ENSEMBLE NO. 1 (1967)**
For violin, alto saxophone, tenor saxophone, French horn, tuba, and piano

> *Duration:*
>> 2 minutes
>
> *First performance:*
>> 1967; Grambling, Louisiana; Grambling College

**24  MUSIC FOR AN EXPERIMENTAL LAB, ENSEMBLE NO. 2 (1967)**
For soprano, flute, 2 trumpets, and piano

> *Text:*
>> "Gloria"
>
> *Unpublished, available from composer*
> *Duration:*
>> 2 minutes
>
> *First performance:*
>> 1968; Frankfort, Kentucky; Kentucky State College

**25** **MUSIC FOR AN EXPERIMENTAL LAB, ENSEMBLE NO. 3 (1970)**
For flute, violin, double bass, and audio generator

> *Unpublished, available from composer*
> *Duration:*
>> 7 minutes

**26** **MUSIC FOR RECORDERS (1972)**
For 2 recorders

> *Unpublished, available from composer*
> *Duration:*
>> 3 minutes
>
> *Two pieces*
> *First performance:*
>> 1973; Weston, Massachusetts; Regis College

**27** **MUSIC FOR TAPE RECORDER NO. 1 (1968)**

> *Unpublished, available from composer*
> *Duration:*
>> 7 minutes

**28** **MUSIC FOR VIOLIN, CELLO, AND PIANO (1972)**

> *To be published by Joshua Corporation, New York*
> *Duration:*
>> 11 minutes
>
> *First performance:*
>> 1972; Amherst, Massachusetts; Amherst College; Julian Olevsky, violin; Leopold Teraspulsky, cello; Estella Olevsky, piano
>
> *Will be recorded by Serenus*

**29** **NAVARAC (1974)**
For jazz ensemble

> *Unpublished, available from composer*
> *Duration:*
>> 6 minutes
>
> *First performance:*
>> 1974; Amherst, Massachusetts; University of Massachusetts Jazz Workshop
>
> *Note:*
>> Written for Jazz Workshop at University of Massachusetts

**30  NIGER SYMPHONY (1975)**
For chamber orchestra

> *Commissioned:*
>> By Hartford Chamber Orchestra, Hartford, Massachusetts
> *To be published by Joshua Corporation, New York*
> *Duration:*
>> 13 minutes 30 seconds
> *In two parts*
> *First performance:*
>> July 1975; Hartford, Massachusetts, Hartford Chamber Orchestra;
>> Daniel Parker, conductor
> *Will be recorded by Serenus*

**31  ONE DOZEN ROCKS, INC. (1971)**
For jazz ensemble

> *Unpublished, available from composer*
> *Duration:*
>> 5 minutes 15 seconds
> *First performance:*
>> 1971; Amherst, Massachusetts; University of Massachusetts
>> Jazz Workshop
> *Note:*
>> Written for Jazz Workshop at University of Massachusetts

**32  OVERTURE TO A DANCE (1961)**
For concert band

> *Duration:*
>> 10 minutes 30 seconds
> *First performance:*
>> 1962; Marshall, Texas; Wiley College
> *Note:*
>> Short analysis in: Everett, Thomas. "Concert Band Music by
>> Black-American Composers," in *The Black Perspective in Music*,
>> vol. 6, no. 2, Fall 1978, pp. 143-50.

**33  PASSACAGLIA FOR BRASS QUINTET (1950)**

> *To be published by Joshua Corporation, New York*
> *Duration:*
>> 4 minutes
> *First performance*
>> 1950; Marshall Texas; Wiley College

**34  PASSACAGLIA FOR ORGAN IN BAROQUE STYLE (1972)**

>>*Duration:*
>>4 minutes

**35  PASTORALE FOR WIND ENSEMBLE (1974)**

>>*Commissioned:*
>>By The Belchertown Music Crusaders
>>*To be published by Joshua Corporation, New York*
>>*Duration:*
>>8 minutes
>>*Note:*
>>>Short analysis in: Everett, Thomas. "Concert Band Music by
>>>Black-American Composers," in *The Black Perspective in Music,*
>>>vol. 6, no. 2, Fall 1978, pp. 143-50

**36  PHANTASY AND ALLEGRO FOR VIOLA AND PIANO (1962)**

>>*Publication:*
>>New York: Southern Music Publishers
>>*Duration:*
>>11 minutes
>>*First performance:*
>>>1962; Iowa City, Iowa; University of Iowa; William Preucil, viola;
>>>William Dopman, piano

**37  POEMS FOR PIANO (1970)**

>>*Dedication:*
>>To Dwight Peltzer
>>*Unpublished, available from composer*
>>*Duration:*
>>17 minutes
>>*First performance:*
>>>1971; New York City; Carnegie Recital Hall; Dwight Peltzer, piano

**38  A PRAYER IN FAITH, PSALMS (1960)**
For voice (baritone) and piano

>>*Text:*
>>>Bible, Old Testament

*Duration:*
> 5 minutes
*First performance:*
> 1973; Weston, Massachusetts; Regis College

**39   QUARTET FOR FLUTE, CLARINET, BASSOON, AND CELLO (1952)**

*Unpublished, available from composer*
*Duration:*
> 8 minutes
*Three movements*
*First performance:*
> 1952; Iowa City, Iowa; University of Iowa
*Note:*
> Master's thesis

**40   QUINTET FOR FOUR WOODWINDS AND PERCUSSION (1963)**
For flute, oboe, clarinet, French horn, and percussion

*Publication:*
> New York: Southern Music Publishers
*Duration:*
> 14 minutes
*First performance:*
> 1971; Amherst, Massachusetts; University of Massachusetts
*Note:*
> Ph.D. dissertation; abstract in *Dissertation Abstracts* XXIV, 6, 2513

**41   REFLECTIONS (1973)**
For medium voice and piano

*Unpublished, available from composer*
*Duration:*
> 4 minutes

**42   RING SHOUT CONCERTO FOR PERCUSSIONIST AND ORCHESTRA (1973-1974)**

*Dedication:*
> To Max Roach

*Duration:*
20 minutes
*In three parts*
*First performance:*
1974; Amherst, Massachusetts; University of Massachusetts
Symphony Orchestra; Max Roach, percussion

**43    SATURN (1978)**
For jazz ensemble

*Unpublished, available from composer*
*Duration:*
8 minutes

**44    SEASONS (1972-1973)**
For women's (SSA) chorus, cello, and percussion

*Text:*
By Floyd Barbour
*Commissioned:*
By Regis College Glee Club
*Unpublished, available from composer*
*Duration:*
10 minutes
*Contents:*
1. Spring (unaccompanied)
2. Summer (with cello, tamborine, triangle, and rattle)
3. Autumn (with bells, gong, and cymbal)
4. Winter (with cello)
*First performance:*
1973; Weston, Massachusetts; Regis College
*Notes:*
Sections can be performed separately
Percussion instruments can be played by choir members

**45    SECRETS OF THE AFRICAN BAOBOB (1976)**
Variations for modern dance/ballet
For jazz orchestra

*Unpublished, available from composer*

*Duration:*
>10 minutes

*First performance:*
>1976; Amherst, Massachusetts; University of Massachusetts Fine Arts Center

**46  SEQUENCES AND BURLESQUE (1966)**
For string orchestra

*Duration:*
>5 minutes 30 seconds

*First performance:*
>1966; Grambling, Louisiana; Grambling College

*Notes:*
>Written for Grambling College String Ensemble
>For student ensemble

**47  SETON CONCERTO FOR TRUMPET (1973)**
For jazz ensemble

*Commissioned:*
>By Richard Williams

*Unpublished, available from composer*
*Duration:*
>8 minutes

**48  SHOWPIECES FOR VIOLA, THREE (1966)**

*Unpublished, available from composer*
*Duration:*
>4 minutes 30 seconds

*Note:*
>Written for the composer

**49  SONGS FOR SOPRANO AND PIANO, TWO (1967-1968)**

*Texts:*
>By Hilda Deal and Willie K. Frazier

*Durations:*
>No. 1–2 minutes; No. 2–2 minutes 45 seconds

*Contents:*
>1. Enogod
>2. Me

*First performance:*
>1973; Weston, Massachusetts, Regis College

**50** **SONGS FROM SHADOWS AND DISTANCE NOWHERE, THREE (1971)**
For unaccompanied voice (tenor)

> *Text:*
>> By Langston Hughes
>
> *Commissioned:*
>> By Ralph K. Williams
>
> *To be published by Joshua Corporation, New York*
> *Durations:*
>> No. 1—1 minute 30 seconds; No. 2—2 minutes; No. 3—3 minutes
>
> *Contents:*
> 1. Hope
> 2. Juliet
> 3. Drum
>
> *First performance:*
>> May 26, 1974; Washington, D. C.; National Gallery; Ralph K.
>> Williams, tenor

**51** **SPIRITUAL CYCLE (1978)**
For soprano and orchestra

> *Text:*
>> By Robert Hayden (*Angle of Ascent*)
>
> *Commissioned:*
>> By the Bernstein Festival
>
> *Unpublished, available from composer*
> *Duration:*
>> 15 minutes
>
> *Contents: 3 spirituals:*
> 1. On Lookout Mountain
> 2. Lord Riot
> 3. And All the Atoms Cry Aloud
>
> *First performance:*
>> Summer 1978; Amherst, Massachusetts; University of
>> Massachusetts; Bernstein Festival of American Music

**52** **SPIRITUALS FOR CHORUS AND BRASS CHOIR, FIVE (1976)**

> *Text:*
>> By Gwendolyn Brooks
>
> *To be published by Joshua Corporation, New York*
> *Duration:*
>> 20 minutes

*Contents:*
1. Oh, I'm Gonna Sing
2. The Urgency
3. Salve Salvage in the Spin
4. All About are the Cold Places
5, The Time

*First performance:*
> (Nos. 1, 3, 5) Summer 1976; University of Massachusetts Chorale on European tour

**53   STRING TRIO (1961)**

> *Duration:*
> > 4 minutes 45 seconds
>
> *First performance:*
> > 1961; Iowa City, Iowa; University of Iowa

**54   SYMPHONIC SPIRITUALS, THREE (1978)**
For orchestra

> *Unpublished, available from composer*
> *Duration:*
> > 11 minutes 30 seconds
>
> *Contents:*
> 1. We Shall Overcome
> 2. Deep River
> 3, Swing Low, Sweet Chariot
>
> *Recording:*
> > Nos. 2 and 3 to be recorded by Columbia

**55   SYMPHONY IN THREE MOVEMENTS (NACIRFA NROH) (1969–**

> *Work in progress*

**THREE CHORALE SETTINGS FOR ORGAN, IN BAROQUE STYLE.** *See* **CHORALE SETTINGS FOR ORGAN, IN BAROQUE STYLE, THREE**

**THREE MOVEMENTS FOR PIANO.** *See* **MOVEMENTS FOR PIANO, THREE**

**56**  **THREE PLUS ONE (1969)**
For clarinet, electronic tape, violin, and guitar

>*Duration:*
>>7 minutes 30 seconds
>
>*First performance:*
>>1969; Frankfort, Kentucky; Kentucky State College


**THREE SHOWPIECES FOR VIOLA.** *See* **SHOWPIECES FOR VIOLA, THREE**


**THREE SONGS FROM SHADOWS AND DISTANCE NOWHERE.** *See* **SONGS FROM SHADOWS AND DISTANCE NOWHERE, THREE**


**THREE SYMPHONIC SPIRITUALS.** *See* **SYMPHONIC SPIRITUALS, THREE**


**TWO SONGS FOR SOPRANO AND PIANO.** *See* **SONGS FOR SOPRANO AND PIANO, TWO**


**57**  **VARIANTS (1979-**

>*On a theme by John Coltrane (Naima)*
>*Work in progress*

*APPENDIX*

Numbers in **boldface** *refer to entry numbers in each composer's WORKS.*
*ARRANGEMENTS, indicated by* \*arr.,
*are found at the end of each composer's WORKS.*

315

## CHORUS AND INSTRUMENTS
(except with only piano/organ)

## CHORUS AND ORCHESTRA

## CHORUS AND PIANO/ORGAN

## CLARINET

## LIST OF PUBLISHERS

| Publishers | Composers |
|---|---|
| AMERICAN COMPOSERS ALLIANCE<br>  (Composers Facsimile Edition)<br>170 W. 74th St.<br>New York, N. Y. 10023 | Moore, Dorothy R.<br>Tillis |
| BELWIN/MILLS PUB. CORP.<br>  (Now combined with E. B. Marks)<br>25 Deshon Dr.<br>Melville, N. Y. 11746 | Boatner<br>Hailstork |
| *Affiliate*  FRANCO COLOMBO | |
| BOOSEY & HAWKES, INC.<br>30 W. 57th St.<br>New York, N. Y. 10019 | Clark |
| BOURNE CO.<br>1212 Avenue of the Americas<br>New York, N. Y. 10036 | Bonds<br>Clark |

CHANTRY MUSIC PRESS, INC.
32-34 North Center St.
Springfield, Ohio 45501
*Affiliate*   GAMBLE-HINGED MUSIC CO.


CHAPPELL & CO., INC.                    Bonds
609 5th Avenue
New York, N. Y. 10017


COMPOSERS FACSIMILE EDITION. *See*
AMERICAN COMPOSERS ALLIANCE


CRESCENDO MUSIC SALES CO.               Hailstork
P. O. Box 395
8 Bunting Ln.
Naperville, Illinois 60540
*Affiliate*   FEMA MUSIC PUBLISHERS


OLIVER DITSON                           Boatner
*Affiliate of*   THEODORE PRESSER


EUROPEAN-AMERICAN MUSIC PUB.            Harris
P. O. Box 2124
Hackensack, New Jersey 07606


FEMA MUSIC PUBLISHERS                   Hailstork
*Affiliate of*   CRESCENDO MUSIC SALES CO.


CARL FISCHER INC.                       Bonds
56-62 Cooper Sq.
New York, N. Y. 10003
*Affiliate*   R. D. ROW MUSIC CO.

| | | |
|---|---|---|
| | J. FISCHER & BROS. | Ryder |
| *Affiliate of* | BELWIN/MILLS | |

H. T. FITZSIMONS CO., INC.       Dawson
615 N. LaSalle St.
Chicago, Illinois 60610

SAM FOX PUB. CO., INC.       Bonds
P. O. Box 850       Furman
Valley Forge, Pennsylvania 19482

GALAXY MUSIC CORP.       Boatner
2121 Broadway       Bonds
New York, N. Y. 10023

GAMBLE-HINGED MUSIC CO.       Dawson
*Affiliate of*   CHANTRY MUSIC PRESS, INC.

GENERAL MUSIC PUB. CO., INC.       Tillis
Box 267
Hastings-on-Hudson, N. Y. 10709

HAMMOND MUSIC (Boatner Associates)    Boatner
76 W. 69th St.
New York, N. Y. 10023

HANDY BROS.       Bonds
200 W. 72nd St.       Clark
New York, N. Y. 10023       Ryder

HINSHAW MUSIC INC.       Furman
P. O. Box 470       Hailstork
Chapel Hill, North Carolina 27514

|  | JOSHUA CORP. | Tillis |
| *Subsidiary of* | GENERAL MUSIC | |

|  | NEIL A. KJOS MUSIC CO. | Clark |
|  | 4382 Jutland Dr. | Dawson |
|  | San Diego, California 92117 | |
|  | *or* | |
|  | 525 Busse Highway | |
|  | Park Ridge, Illinois 60068 | |
| *Affiliates* | TUSKEGEE MUSIC PRESS | |
|  | PALLMA MUSIC CO. | |

LAWSON-GOULD MUSIC PUB., INC.  Furman
866 Third Ave.
New York, N. Y. 10022

EDWARD B. MARKS MUSIC CORP.  Boater
  (Now combined with Belwin/Mills)  Clark
1790 Broadway
New York, N. Y. 10019

McAFEE MUSIC CORP.  Boatner
300 E. 59th St., Suite 1202
New York, N. Y.

MERCURY MUSIC  Bonds
c/o THEODORE PRESSER

MUTUAL MUSIC SOCIETY  Bonds
c/o CHAPPELL & CO., INC.

OXFORD UNIVERSITY PRESS, INC.  Furman
200 Madison Ave.
New York, N. Y. 10016

| | | |
|---|---|---|
| | PALLMA MUSIC CO. | Clark |
| *Affiliate of* | NEIL A. KJOS MUSIC CO. | |
| | | |
| | PEER-SOUTHERN CORP.<br>1740 Broadway<br>New York, N. Y. 10019 | |
| | | |
| | PIEDMONT MUSIC | Hailstork |
| *Affiliate of* | E. B. MARKS MUSIC CORP. | |
| | | |
| | POWERS PUBLISHERS<br>Seattle, Washington | Logan |
| | | |
| | THEODORE PRESSER | Bonds |
| *Rental works* | 111 W. 57th St. | Cunningham |
| | New York, N. Y. 10016 | |
| *Published works* | Bryn Mawr, Pennsylvania 19010 | |
| | | |
| | REMICK MUSIC CORP. | Dawson |
| *Affiliate of* | WARNER BROS. PUB., INC. | |
| | | |
| | G. RICORDI & CO. | Boatner |
| *Represented by* | ASSOCIATED MUSIC PUBLISHERS<br>866 Third Ave.<br>New York, N. Y. 10022 | |
| | | |
| | R. D. ROW MUSIC CO. | Bonds |
| *Affiliate of* | CARL FISCHER INC. | Ryder |
| | | |
| | G. SCHIRMER INC.<br>866 Third Ave.<br>New York, N. Y. 10022 | Ryder |

SHAPIRO, BERNSTEIN & CO., INC. Cunningham
666 Fifth Ave.
New York, N. Y. 10019


SHAWNEE PRESS, INC. Clark
Delaware Water Gap, Pennsylvania 18327


SILVER BURDETTE CO. Clark
Columbia Road
Morristown, New Jersey 07960


SOLO MUSIC, INC. Bonds
4708 Van Noord Ave.
Sherman Oaks, California 91423


    SOUTHERN MUSIC PUB. CO., INC. Dickerson
*Part of* PEER-SOUTHERN CORP. Tillis


SUNDAY SCHOOL PUB. BOARD, Boatner
  NATIONAL BAPTIST CONVENTION
330 Charlotte Ave.
Nashville, Tennessee 37201


    TUSKEGEE MUSIC PRESS Dawson
*Distributed by* NEIL A. KJOS MUSIC CO.


WARNER BROS. PUB., INC. Dawson
75 Rockefeller Plaza
New York, N. Y. 10019


    WITMARK & SONS Cunningham
*Affiliate of* WARNER BROS. PUB., INC.